THE TOP
100
MIRACLES
OF THE BIBLE

THE TOP
100
MIRACLES
OF THE BIBLE

what they are and what they mean to you today

PAMELA McQUADE

BARBOUR
PUBLISHING

Cover image © The DesignWorks Group

Published by Barbour Publishing, Inc., P.O. Box 719, Uhrichsville, Ohio 44683
www.barbourbooks.com

Our mission is to publish and distribute inspirational products offering exceptional value and biblical encouragement to the masses.

Member of the
Evangelical Christian
Publishers Association

Printed in the United States of America.

CONTENTS

INTRODUCTION

What is a miracle? We tend to use the word rather loosely, to describe anything from our getting across a busy street safely to the birth of a child. Strictly speaking, miracles are not simply wonderful things that happen, like the birth of a baby, though through such events we may begin to understand God's miraculous work of creation. Real miracles are events that break the laws of nature and require God's direct action.

Miracles do not appear in every book of the Bible. They tend to come in clumps, mostly during the Creation and during the lives of Moses, Elijah, Elisha, and Jesus, and again during the apostles' ministries in the book of Acts.

Nor does scripture describe miracles with one word. They are variously called "signs," "wonders," "mighty works," or "works." These words describe what the miracle does, the purpose God has for working it. A sign evidences God's presence. From it, observers clearly understand that He, and not a human, is taking action. Wonders cause those who see them to be awed by what God has done. And mighty works show God's power and authority in this world.

In these pages, when I speak of a man working a miracle, of course I do not mean he did it on his own. All true miracles come from God and are empowered by Him. People can do many things, but they cannot make a miracle happen. Those involved in biblical miracles are God's servants, and His power flows through them when the amazing events take place. A real servant of God would never say otherwise.

While most miracles are positive, some, like the plagues inflicted upon Egypt, are examples of God's judgment. God uses miracles to protect and encourage His people, but He also uses them to show both believers and unbelievers the error of their ways and the authority that is His. Often miracles so influence those who see them that they recognize their sin and turn to the Lord in faith. But that is not a universal response.

Likewise, some miracles are focused on an individual while others address a broad number of people—frequently the whole Jewish nation. Elisha and Jesus performed many miracles that affected one person: an intimate healing that seemed to influence only that individual. But events like the parting of the Red Sea or the feeding of the five thousand touched a multitude. The scope of miracles clearly shows that God cares about those things in our lives that we deal with personally and those that influence our society or our world. Yet the biblical miracle we consider unimportant may have changed one person's life and made that person touch his or her world effectively for the Lord. Rarely do we see that side of the story in scripture—only in eternity will we know the full impact a single miracle had.

Several Gospels frequently tell the same miracle stories. To make this book more readable, I have rarely identified the parallel Gospel passages. Most details of the story that do not appear in the quoted passage should be in the other Gospels. Careful students may want to check a study Bible to identify the parallel passages and read all the information scripture provides about each miracle.

It has been popular with unbelievers through the centuries to deny or denigrate miracles. Doubters have tried to bring the scriptures down to their own level by implying that of course such things never could have happened. The biblical writers, they would claim, made up or expanded on the original events. These doubters' earthbound view of God appears nowhere in scripture for a good reason: to believe in miracles requires faith, and those without faith will never understand the events portrayed in the Old and New Testaments. Those who try to eradicate miracles from the scripture lose all faith's joy, for they are left with little more than moral rules to live by.

CREATION'S BEGINNING

In the beginning God created the heavens and the earth.
Now the earth was formless and empty, darkness was
over the surface of the deep, and the Spirit of
God was hovering over the waters.
GENESIS 1:1–2

Of all the miracles of the Bible, this may be the most stunning. It certainly counts as a miracle—something far beyond what humanity could do, a disruption of the natural order. What natural order existed before God created heaven and earth? Nothingness.

Scripture's account starts with the rather matter-of-fact description "In the beginning God created the heaven and the earth" (Genesis 1:1 KJV). Those few words tell us a lot about God and His work in Creation while cloaking our planet's beginnings in a great mystery. Creation didn't just happen. Some authorless Big Bang didn't simply explode on the universe. But out of a seemingly blank emptiness, life appeared. All that existed prior to this event was God, a fact scripture takes for granted.

God didn't take old matter and refashion it. He required not so much as a molecule to start with. In a specific moment, out of a great emptiness, life took form as He "call[ed] into existence the things that do not exist" (Romans 4:17 ESV). In a flash God ignited the new creation. The word translated "God" is the Hebrew word *elohim*, the majestic plural that indicates the whole Trinity is at work in this moment. In case we miss it, Genesis 1:2 tells us the life-giving Spirit hovered over the waters. Nor does the New Testament leave us in doubt that Jesus took part in the event (see John 1:1, 3, 10; Colossians 1:15–17).

The few words that begin Creation's story provide us with important information. This is a planned event, begun by an infinitely powerful Being, who was able to organize everything from the smallest details to the whole massive grand plan. Instead of leaving us hanging in the air, believing life always existed or has no rhyme or reason, God gives us a view of how life began.

When did this event happen? Scripture doesn't define it by as-yet-uncreated years. That indefinite timetable may irritate our desire for scientific understanding, but how else can a work that began before time be described? God's Word accurately details the main events that took place under His hand.

Genesis 1 doesn't give us the roiling, chaotic description of the new world that some scientists offer, because it's not the totally out-of-control event they imagine. God managed everything, no matter how unorganized it seemed. Creation might not have been a neat period, but it was not about to fly off on an unexpected course, either. As scripture shows us, creative order prevailed as God orchestrated each event.

How do we know it happened this way? Scripture does not refer us to scientific treatises or hard-and-fast proof. "By faith," it declares, "we understand that the worlds were framed by the word of God" (Hebrews 11:3 NKJV). The Old Testament is not interested in scientific theories any more than it was in the pagan creation stories of its day. Just as the multiple deities of the Greeks and other nations could not impact God's account of His doings, colorful scientific theories need not disrupt our faith. Chance did not begin this world or the universes beyond it: God did.

The ancient Hebrews may have had it over us in understanding God's message. We tend to see the Creation story in scientific terms. But in a world that knew nothing of black holes, quarks, and other scientific mysteries, they turned to spiritual mysteries instead. As we seek hard-and-fast "realities," perhaps we miss out on the spiritual realities that overwhelm the best scientific research humankind can do.

But here begin the greatest spiritual realities of this world. God graciously created a world just for humans, a stage on which the salvation drama would be acted out. The playhouse is prepared, the first actors will be placed on it. Life has begun!

TURNING ON THE LIGHT

*And God said, "Let there be light," and there was light. God
saw that the light was good, and he separated the light from
the darkness. God called the light "day," and the darkness
he called "night." And there was evening,
and there was morning—the first day.*

GENESIS 1:3–5

God speaks, and over the formless earth appears light, a symbol
of both Himself and the salvation that is yet to take place for
humankind. Where did the light come from? Some scholars
maintain it was a light emanating from God, while others cor-
relate this passage to verse 14 and the creation of the heavenly
bodies. Whichever is true, God used His words to create light
and then separated it from darkness, creating the first day
and night. Looking at the newborn light, God pronounced
it good.

We may balk at knowing only that God's speech initiated
the creative power, directed by His own will. But scripture
focuses not on the *how* of Creation but the *who* of the
Creator. From His mind leapt this element of Creation that
will forever describe Himself. With this concrete picture, we
begin to understand our Lord. He "turns on the light" in our
own souls, and darkness separates itself from us, though in
this life it never entirely disappears. With the daylight turned
on in our hearts, we can serve Him day and night.

SEPARATING THE WATERS

And God said, "Let there be an expanse between the waters
to separate water from water." So God made the expanse and
separated the water under the expanse from the water above
it. And it was so. God called the expanse "sky." And there
was evening, and there was morning—the second day.
GENESIS 1:6–8

On the second day, God began a serious reorganization of His formless creation. A brand-new sky, along with its cloud-bound waters, separated from earthly waters below. Yet still there was no sun. This was only the beginning of a vast creation project. God started at the top of the earthly realm.

Describing God's glory, David portrayed this day of creation as such: "He stretches out the heavens like a tent" (Psalm 104:2). Rain-bearing clouds rose above the earth's firmament for the first time. Below lay the mere beginnings of oceans, seas, and rivers.

When we look upward, what does the sky remind us of? Will fluffy clouds, a clear sky, or signs of a storm coming remind us of God's glory and the miracle He commanded on that second day? Let's remind ourselves that our planet was once a huge void: light and darkness, sky, oceans, and rivers all washed together. From this, God created an expanse that warns us of coming storms, sends us rain, or simply delights us on a balmy summer day.

Isn't our Creator glorious?

SOMETHING TO STAND ON

*And God said, "Let the water under the sky be gathered to
one place, and let dry ground appear." And it was so. God
called the dry ground "land," and the gathered waters he
called "seas." And God saw that it was good.*
GENESIS 1:9–10

This is an especially important miracle for those of us who
walk on earth, for had God not gathered the sea in one place
and raised the land above it, there would have been no place
for human or animal life. Even birds might have gotten rather
wing weary, never having a place to alight, and what would
they have eaten, with no bountiful earth to sustain them?

Instead of creating one large oceanographic planet,
on creation's third day God sank the oceans, rivers, and
even streams into the earth. Land rose up, in mountains,
jagged shores, and barely above-sea-level flats. Though this
vegetationless land had yet to look like the world we recognize,
God's orderly creation had begun to develop, and the world
became a place to stand on for all the life yet to come.

Have you thanked God today for having a place to stand?
Whether He created large masses of land or small, delicate
islands, He was thinking of you and the other creatures that
would put their feet there someday.

THE PLANT KINGDOM

*Then God said, "Let the earth bring forth grass,
the herb that yields seed, and the fruit tree that
yields fruit according to its kind, whose seed
is in itself, on the earth"; and it was so.*
GENESIS 1:11 NKJV

As the third day continued, God covered the land with all kinds of vegetation, grass, and trees. Annual and perennial flowers and vegetables appeared; the limbs of massive oaks and slender beeches crisscrossed the sky. And for the first time, God gave part of creation the ability to continue His creative process: all the plants bore seeds. That reproduction must have begun immediately to support the new world. Each plant contained a genetic code so it would reproduce in keeping with its own variety. Trees would not bring forth grass, nor flowers produce grain.

While the immovable foundations of the earth would always be fixed, plant growth, which provided food for humans and beasts and a home for the birds of the air, would vary every year. God's ongoing provision for all the earth was established in a way that required dependence on Him. And the ancient peoples appreciated this as their harvests came in well one year and were pitiful the next. Vegetation had the ability to remind people of the Creator and His call on their lives.

Do we too remember that call?

LET THERE BE LIGHT

And God said, "Let there be lights in the expanse
of the sky to separate the day from the night, and let them
serve as signs to mark seasons and days and years,
and let them be lights in the expanse of the sky to give
light on the earth." And it was so.

GENESIS 1:14–15

Imagine yourself, early on the fourth day, standing on the earth as God created the moon and stars. The velvety dark mantle above the earth would suddenly have shown soft pinpricks of light as far-flung universes came into being. Then the sun would have risen with its brighter light, warming the vegetation beneath and providing it with the ability to grow.

But the most amazing miracle would have been that the sun was placed in a perfect position that allowed life to exist and thrive. Had it been closer, Earth would have overheated and been unable to sustain plants, animals, and humans. Farther away, and it would have been too cold to sustain this delicate balance of existence we take for granted.

Before Moses' era, paganism overtook most of the earth, and the sun and moon became deities to many people. So God does not even name them when He transmits this part of the Word. Scripture simply tells us the sun, moon, and stars were made to define human lives, separating day and night and identifying the seasons. This would have been particularly important to ancient believers, as the Jews told time through a lunar calendar.

Yet God specifically prohibited His people from following their neighbors and worshiping or fearing the heavenly bodies (see Deuteronomy 4:19; Isaiah 40:26). The sun and moon and stars were meant to encourage worship of the Lord God, not to be used as pagan gods or a focus of occult practices.

The heavenly creation described in Genesis 1:14–19 is to provide light for the earth and act as a timekeeper for humankind. These bodies in no way rule the earth, for that is God's job. Though they are not the light of God, the sun, moon, and stars illuminate our way in a purely earthly manner. In eternity there will be no need for them, as the New Jerusalem will be lit by God's glory (see Revelation 21:23).

So let's enjoy the lights' beauty here on earth, when daylight begins to touch the dark sky with delicate color or slips into night with an incredible range of blues, rising from the horizon in ever-darkening hues. God has given the stars and planets to delight us as we worship Him faithfully. So let's rejoice in the miracle of this day of creation as we worship the Creator.

ABUNDANT LIFE

*Then God said, "Let the waters abound with an abundance
of living creatures, and let birds fly above the earth across the
face of the firmament of the heavens." So God created great sea
creatures and every living thing that moves, with which the
waters abounded, according to their kind, and every winged bird
according to its kind. And God saw that it was good.*
GENESIS 1:20–21 NKJV

The waters God had created lay empty, except perhaps for
seaweed and other vegetation. No seagulls flew across the
ocean surface, no seabirds dive-bombed from toothlike rocks.
Fish never broke the ocean waves.

Again God spoke, and these waters teemed with new
life: whales and fish, and even sharks. Through the sky above,
the birds darted, and all had a purpose in God's plan. God
gave all the creatures the ability to reproduce, just as He had
done for the plants. He blessed them all, commanding them
to multiply and fill the seas and sky.

As we read of God's inventive creation on the fifth day,
are we reminded that it is ours to care for and enjoy? Let us
treasure the gift given in this miracle of creation. It's part of
the abundant life He offers.

CREATURES GREAT AND SMALL

And God said, "Let the land produce living creatures according to their kinds: livestock, creatures that move along the ground, and wild animals, each according to its kind."
GENESIS 1:24

When He'd filled the seas and skies with creatures, God didn't stop. Before Him lay the land—empty except for vegetation and birds nesting in the trees. Nothing roamed the land. So God began to fill His landscape with all kinds of creatures. Cows and horses; carnivorous tigers and lions and bears; gentle deer and antelope; and snakes, lizards, and other creeping creatures were placed in their proper habitats. On savannahs, mountains, and in wetlands, animals designed for each environment appeared.

Think about the amazing detail involved in this creation. Creatures from intriguing polar bears and penguins, who inhabit the frigid ends of the earth, to ordinary tree-climbing squirrels and earthbound chipmunks were designed specially for the places in which they'd live.

But God had another consideration in the creation of the animals. He made some animals clean and others unclean. For fallen humans they became a picture of holiness—Jews were to avoid eating the unclean animals. And God would give humankind stewardship over all the creatures He'd created, from elephants to skinks.

God teaches us much about His world through the creatures He put in it. We're awed by the details of His Creation and challenged to care for it well. What lessons have you learned from the animals God made?

MADE IN THE IMAGE

Then God said, "Let us make man in our image, in our likeness, and let them rule over the fish of the sea and the birds of the air, over the livestock, over all the earth, and over all the creatures that move along the ground." So God created man in his own image, in the image of God he created him; male and female he created them. God blessed them and said to them, "Be fruitful and increase in number; fill the earth and subdue it."
GENESIS 1:26–28

As whales swam in the ocean; parrots, kingfishers, and sparrows flew the skies; and buffalo stampeded on the plains, God perfected His Creation. Though you might doubt it looking at the world today, as He created man He was about to come to the pinnacle of His creative process. After the Father, Son, and Holy Spirit considered together the form this creation should take, Adam was made in the Creator's image.

This new creation was made not in a physical likeness of God, but with a soul, to have communion with Him. Theologians have debated just what being made in God's image entails, but at the very least this first man had attributes the animals lacked. He had a larger ability to think and communicate, and he had a soul. Of all the beings on earth, he was the most like God, while still only a distant reflection of His nature.

God also made humans in male and female forms, though Eve's creation account is detailed after Adam's. Before Eve was brought into being, God gave Adam dominion over the entire world. He was to rule over the animals, birds, and sea creatures. No creature had more authority than he, though many had more physical strength. This somewhat puny being was to have command over powerful elephants and alligators. Together, Adam and Eve were commanded to fill and subdue the earth. As part of their God-given task, they too were to be fruitful and multiply, for God was just beginning to fill the earth with all the good things He had created.

What must this couple have thought, standing, newly created, in a garden filled with beautiful plants, the noise of the animals and birds ringing in their ears? As they looked at the bright, untouched Creation, did they feel the weight of God's trust on them? Did they understand the importance of the command He had given them? Everything in the garden was new, including the couple in charge of it.

God had made Adam and Eve and declared them good. Doubtless they were up to the task. At this point, it never would have occurred to the only humans in the world to do wrong by the plants and animals or to disobey God. The ideas of wrong and disobedience had yet to be thought of. Theirs was a perfect world, in tune with God.

When they took up their new mission, did Adam talk to the animals while Eve picked fruit for breakfast? Whatever they did, it was the start of a wonderful existence in which the humans used each moment to glorify their Creator.

Are you awed when you think about the creation of the first man and woman? Have you thought about what it meant to God to create the height of His Creation? How does that make you feel about the fact that God made you, too?

Because humans are made in the image of God, Christians have a high view of the value of other people. How should this make a difference in your life?

A BEAUTIFUL CREATION

So Adam gave names to all cattle, to the birds of the air, and to every beast of the field. But for Adam there was not found a helper comparable to him. And the LORD God caused a deep sleep to fall on Adam, and he slept; and He took one of his ribs, and closed up the flesh in its place. Then the rib which the LORD God had taken from man He made into a woman, and He brought her to the man. And Adam said: "This is now bone of my bones and flesh of my flesh; she shall be called Woman, because she was taken out of Man." Therefore a man shall leave his father and mother and be joined to his wife, and they shall become one flesh. And they were both naked, the man and his wife, and were not ashamed.

GENESIS 2:20–25 NKJV

After God introduces the subject of the creation of man, scripture gives us the details of Eve's introduction to the world. Once Adam, who got to find a name for each creature, had finished this first task (Can you imagine what Eve thought when she heard of Adam's creativity in this direction? "So tell me, why did you name it a *hippopotamus*?"), it became apparent just one thing was missing: a mate for Adam. So God sedated the first man, delved into his side, took one of his ribs, and made a wife for him. Eve must have been some beautiful woman, considering the poem Adam immediately created as he named her *woman*.

This couple was just perfect for each other. The goodness of God's creation extended to their relationship. No divisions, no doubts about each other, no "battle of the sexes" existed in the Garden of Eden. From the very first, scripture also makes it clear that monogamy is God's design, for the two are designed to be one flesh—not merely connected, but related in the most intimate way. They were completely intimate, with no shame dividing them. Nor did anything come between them and their Creator.

But this picture of marital harmony was not to last long, for even if Adam and Eve had not thought of disobeying God, Satan had. The crafty fallen angel, taking on the form of a snake, started asking Eve a question—one designed to separate her from God. His ploy of raising doubts in her mind worked, and little by little, his temptation began to appeal to her. Instead of saying, "Let's ask Adam what he thinks," Eve made a selfish choice. Once her interest in the only forbidden fruit in the garden piqued, she picked some and offered it to her husband, too.

In a moment, the miracle of the pinnacle of creation became deeply marred, and sin entered the once-idyllic world. Adam and Eve immediately started making leaf loincloths, because they knew they were naked. When God came for a stroll in the garden, the damage to their relationship became apparent. The couple ran from Him for the first time. Separation between God and His creation had begun. And God gave each of the offenders an appropriate punishment. For Adam and Eve, it meant leaving their beautiful garden and living with the sin that broke their intimacy with their Lord.

God made Eve as a wonderful gift for Adam, and Adam appreciated it. But since the fall, marital relationships have become much more challenging. How does the relationship described in the Garden of Eden compare with marriage today? What can people do to appreciate the miracle God did for Adam and bring something of that kind of relationship to their own lives?

Adam and Eve's story not only tells of the blessings God gives but shows the huge change sin makes in our lives. The blessings of a miracle are not indestructible in this fallen world. Let's be careful with the miracles that have touched our lives.

BURNED BUT UNCONSUMED

Now Moses kept the flock of Jethro his father in law,
the priest of Midian: and he led the flock to the backside of the
desert, and came to the mountain of God, even to Horeb. And
the angel of the LORD appeared unto him in a flame of fire out of
the midst of a bush: and he looked, and, behold, the bush burned
with fire, and the bush was not consumed. And Moses said,
I will now turn aside, and see this great sight,
why the bush is not burnt.
EXODUS 3:1–3 KJV

By the time Moses was confronted by a burning bush, he was a man with a history. Adopted by Pharaoh's daughter, he had a cushy life, until he began to understand how the Egyptians abused his own people, the Hebrews. To protect one of his people, Moses killed a man and had to run for his life. Following his escape, he met the daughters of Jethro, married one of them, and became part of the family business. That's how he ended up at the backside of the desert, herding sheep.

On what was probably a fairly ordinary day, Moses led his sheep out to graze. As they moved through the barren landscape, the shepherd looked up and saw an amazing thing: a burning bush that was not consumed by the fire. Curious, Moses went to inspect the plant and was confronted by something even less likely: the angel of the Lord appeared in the bush, and God spoke to him!

God told the stunned shepherd to remove his sandals, for he stood on holy ground. Hiding his face in fear, Moses received the astonishing news that God had a plan for him: Moses would return to Egypt to lead God's people from their oppression and into a new land.

If the bush had seemed spectacular, this news was even more so. God would work through a shepherd to bring about a world-changing plan. For the first time, a nation would escape slavery in the powerful Egyptian Empire. It's not surprising Moses had his doubts about this plan.

Just as the bush was burned but unconsumed, Moses would be. He had much to face from the people he led: doubt, criticism, and rebellion were his lot from them. But because of God's power in him, the prophet was not destroyed by their attitudes.

We, too, need not be consumed by the world if we trust in the Lord alone and seek to serve Him. Do we?

WHAT'S IN YOUR HAND?

And the LORD said unto him, What is that in thine hand?
And he said, A rod. And he said, Cast it on the ground. And he
cast it on the ground, and it became a serpent; and Moses fled
from before it. And the LORD said unto Moses, Put forth thine
hand, and take it by the tail. And he put forth his hand,
and caught it, and it became a rod in his hand.

EXODUS 4:2–4 KJV

If anyone wonders if God has a sense of humor, show them this miracle. God turned Moses' staff into a snake, and the prophet, perhaps not realizing that God was in control even of the slithery creatures, ran away from it. Could the Lord have kept from chuckling?

Worry got Moses into this reptilian situation. The Lord had commanded His prophet to go to Egypt and confront Pharaoh, but Moses feared no one would believe his message. As God showed Moses how to prove the truth of His Word, the prophet leapt away from the fast-moving snake, more afraid of the serpent than any of the Egyptians would ever be. Yet when, at God's command, Moses gingerly picked up the snake, he again held his staff. The former shepherd probably took a good second look at the rod that had been his support for many years.

The snake was more for Moses' and his people's benefit than the Egyptians', who didn't believe it meant anything, even when Moses' snake ate up their own. But knowing that he could prove himself probably meant a lot to the prophet, and when Pharaoh requested a miracle, he was prepared. This miracle also gave Moses' fellow Israelites a clue that what he said was really from God. And the reason God ordained Moses to do this miracle was so that His people would know Him.

At least it should have given Pharaoh one idea about Moses, for a cobra had long adorned the crown of Egypt. With his snake that ate the Egyptian reptiles, Moses was about to become a serious threat to Pharaoh's rule.

God doesn't always prove Himself in miraculous physical ways, as He did in this instance. But He often uses the things that are right in our hands to show His faithfulness to us. With them, we can always be ready to show forth God's truth to those who doubt. In His hand, the common becomes uncommon, and amazing events can happen.

Do you doubt God's ability to work in your life? Ask yourself if the shepherd Moses ever thought he'd be leading a horde of two or three million people out of Egypt and toward the Promised Land.

AN UNPLEASANT MIRACLE

Again, the LORD said to him, "Put your hand inside your cloak."
And he put his hand inside his cloak, and when he took it out,
behold, his hand was leprous like snow. Then God said,
"Put your hand back inside your cloak." So he put his hand
back inside his cloak, and when he took it out, behold,
it was restored like the rest of his flesh.
EXODUS 4:6–7 ESV

God not only gave Moses the ability to turn his staff into a snake, He had a backup plan, a less pleasant miracle. Leprosy was a much-feared disease in this age, and anyone who could heal it would be a wonder worker indeed. His God would be one to look up to and worship faithfully.

God commanded that anyone with leprosy was unclean— separated from others so the illness would not spread. Such a person was also a picture of spiritual unbelief or failure. Anyone who could work this miracle would be someone to follow and respect, for surely this would be God's representative.

Does God have to make us fear Him before we obey? Will only the unpleasant get our attention? Then He will use such a method. But He would rather woo us, calling us into obedience with a gentle voice. Are we listening?

BLOOD EVERYWHERE!

The LORD said to Moses, "Tell Aaron, 'Take your staff and stretch out your hand over the waters of Egypt—over the streams and canals, over the ponds and all the reservoirs'—and they will turn to blood. Blood will be everywhere in Egypt, even in the wooden buckets and stone jars." Moses and Aaron did just as the LORD had commanded. He raised his staff in the presence of Pharaoh and his officials and struck the water of the Nile, and all the water was changed into blood. The fish in the Nile died, and the river smelled so bad that the Egyptians could not drink its water. Blood was everywhere in Egypt.

EXODUS 7:19–21

The prophet and his brother, Aaron, appeared before Pharaoh numerous times. First they politely requested that the Egyptian king allow the Israelites to hold a religious feast in the wilderness. Pharaoh didn't have to think for a minute before he said no to that one; he didn't respect the Lord and didn't like the idea of losing his slaves. Instead, Egypt's ruler punished all the Israelites, increasing their workload by requiring them to make bricks without the strengthening element of straw.

At God's command, the brothers returned to Pharaoh's court to confront him. Aaron's staff turning into a snake didn't get the Egyptians' attention, so God commanded that Moses return a third time to the Pharaoh to initiate the first of ten plagues Egypt would experience at God's hand.

You couldn't say that God hadn't been patient with Pharaoh, but Egypt's ruler had a hard heart when it came to hearing the message.

Since Pharaoh was unlikely to let Moses and his brother into the court, God sent them to the Nile River to confront Pharaoh. The first plague struck at Egypt's lifeblood: the Nile River. This civilization depended on the overflowing river to water its crops, and one of the nation's numerous deities, the god Hapi, was associated with the river and the provision of life for the Egyptians.

When God told Moses to turn the Nile to blood, He struck both a political and religious blow. By disproving the power of Egypt's gods, He showed the powerlessness of their religion and the ruler who was considered one of the gods.

As Aaron lifted and dropped his staff to touch the Nile River, Egyptian life entered a crisis. The water in the entire Nile and in every water-holding wood and stone vessel turned to blood. The fish that once swam in the Nile now lay dead on top of it. The river stank, and no one could drink from it. Everyone had to dig wells along the river for potable water.

In response, the Egyptian magicians turned water into blood—a rather ineffective reaction, since turning blood into water would have been more useful. Some scholars think blood filled the Nile for seven days. Yet because his magicians had turned a small amount of water into blood, or at least made it look like blood, Pharaoh remained unmoved.

Certainly the God whom Moses and Aaron worshiped didn't appeal to Egypt's king. Hard-hearted Pharaoh trusted his foolish magicians. After all, why should Egypt's leader give up believing he was a god because a shepherd claimed he had a better God?

Like many people today, Pharaoh was comfortable in his unbelief. The world seemed to revolve around him, and he liked it that way. There was little room in his life for real truth that confronted his false reality.

When we witness to people who refuse to believe, let's understand that they are caught in Pharaoh's trap. Only God can release them from the hardness of their own hearts. Before we seek to bring the Word to them, we'd be wise to spend time in prayer that seeks to open hearts to Him.

Then the LORD said to Moses, "Tell Aaron, 'Stretch out your hand with your staff over the streams and canals and ponds, and make frogs come up on the land of Egypt.'" So Aaron stretched out his hand over the waters of Egypt, and the frogs came up and covered the land. But the magicians did the same things by their secret arts; they also made frogs come up on the land of Egypt.

EXODUS 8:5–7

A week after Aaron's rod had turned the Nile to blood, he and his brother were back on Pharaoh's doorstep, repeating God's demand to let His people go. But the king refused, so out of the streams, canals, and ponds erupted a superabundance of frogs: frogs in his palace, frogs in his bed, frogs in the houses of his officials and his people. Frogs filled the ovens and kneading troughs, making food production a disaster. Almost every part of daily life must have been affected by this second plague. Along with all those frogs, the king must have heard a lot of complaining, probably from his family, his court officials, and the mobs who wanted to know how he planned to solve this problem.

It must not have taken long for the king to weary of this overabundance of amphibians. And for once, the fact that his magicians had added a few frogs to the mix didn't deter him from wanting to lose all those critters. He called Moses and Aaron to him and begged them to pray for him. Pharaoh was desperate for an end to the crisis.

Moses promised that the next day the frogs would again inhabit only their normal habitat. His goal was to show the king that the Lord was God. When God did what Moses asked, perhaps the king almost wished he hadn't requested the solution. For now he had dead frogs in his palace, in his people's homes, in courtyards and fields. All Egypt stank of dead frogs. But once they were piled up out of reach of his nasal passages, Pharaoh again hardened his heart.

Pharaoh probably didn't see the eruption of frogs into his life as a miracle, but he could certainly appreciate their sudden removal. But once the frogs were dead, maybe it didn't seem like such a big thing. We can relate to Pharaoh's about-face, can't we? For we, too, have begged God for relief from a problem, only to forget all He's done for us when our pain is relieved.

Do we forget God's graces too easily? Is He truly Lord of our lives?

THOSE PESKY GNATS

Then the LORD said to Moses, "Tell Aaron, 'Stretch out your staff and strike the dust of the ground,' and throughout the land of Egypt the dust will become gnats."
EXODUS 8:16

If you've ever been at a gnat-infested picnic, you know the trouble Egypt was in when the Lord commanded that Aaron's staff should inflict a third plague on Egypt. As Aaron's staff hit the ground, gnats as numerous as the dust rose up to annoy both humans and beasts. Small as they were, they were highly irritating. Where could anyone get away from them?

With this plague the Egyptian magicians were foiled. They could not make gnats. Maybe the people of Egypt were glad; after all, who needed any more of the annoying creatures? Nor could the magicians stop the infestation. Finally, they were forced to admit that God had done this. But proud Pharaoh was not convinced.

Insidious as the bugs were, they should have given Pharaoh a message that God was determined to get through to him. We've seen this determination in our own lives, when God has wanted us to understand that the life we've been living is not what He wants. He will continually redirect us until we finally listen.

Is God redirecting us today?

"If you do not let my people go, I will send swarms of flies on you and your officials, on your people and into your houses. The houses of the Egyptians will be full of flies, and even the ground where they are."

EXODUS 8:21

Again Moses appeared at the riverside when Pharaoh was preparing for an agreeable sail. But the news the prophet bore wasn't pleasant: Since gnats didn't have an impact on Pharaoh, God was going to send something larger: swarms of flies, so many they would ruin the land. But to make it clear to the king whose God He was, the Hebrews, living in the land of Goshen, would remain unaffected by the purely Egyptian plague.

When the annoyance became too much, Pharaoh called Moses and his brother back. This time he wanted to negotiate with God. He offered to let the Hebrews sacrifice inside Egypt. When Moses refused, the king offered to let them go into the wilderness, but for less than the three days God had stipulated. Moses agreed to plead with God but warned the king not to cheat again.

Again, Pharaoh gave the predictable response.

God is not One to be bargained with, as Pharaoh would discover. Just as he could not turn God from His purpose, neither can we. Do we try to cheat Him?

CATTLE PROD

*"If you refuse to let them go and continue to hold them back,
the hand of the LORD will bring a terrible plague on your
livestock in the field—on your horses and donkeys and camels
and on your cattle and sheep and goats. But the LORD will make
a distinction between the livestock of Israel and that of Egypt,
so that no animal belonging to the Israelites will die."*
EXODUS 9:2–4

Streams and rivers of blood, frogs, gnats, and flies: None of
these plagues deterred Pharaoh. So God announced that in
one day He would send a fifth, terrible plague that affected
the animals of the land. Again, the Israelites' animals would
remain untouched by the affliction.

Though Pharaoh had enough warning to stop the deaths,
he remained adamant, and the cattle fell throughout the
land. What a health problem that must have caused! And it
certainly would have seriously damaged Egypt's economy.

As Egypt's ruler remained hard-hearted before God's
prodding, the Lord began to touch his nation's economy.
Where formerly the vegetation had been harmed, now the
country's ability to produce milk and meat had been killed
off. Small farmers and wealthy landowners alike saw their
futures destroyed as their most valuable animals died.

Standing adamant against God is never profitable.
Without His blessing, we harm both our livelihoods and our
spiritual well-being.

THE FEEL OF SIN

So they took soot from a furnace and stood before Pharaoh.
Moses tossed it into the air, and festering boils broke out
on men and animals. The magicians could not stand
before Moses because of the boils that were
on them and on all the Egyptians.
EXODUS 9:10–11

In the sixth plague, God commanded Moses to do a strange thing. Picking up soot from a furnace, he tossed it into the air, and painful, debilitating boils broke out on man and the few beasts left in Egypt. Just about every living thing must have been in agony. Neither could Pharaoh's court stand before it, as the men the king depended on for spiritual counsel failed him. Still, probably covered himself with the painful, pus-filled eruptions, Pharaoh stood firm in his hard-heartedness.

Anyone who consistently stands against God will suffer increasing pain, spiritual or physical. Here God made Pharaoh and his people feel the pain of sin in their own bodies. There was no way to escape or forget about God's message.

Not all physical problems come from sin, but illness is certainly something we need to discuss with God. Have we brought it on ourselves by our bad habits or bad attitudes? Do we need to seek Him and ask for clean hearts, as well as clean bodies?

When Moses stretched out his staff toward the sky,
the LORD sent thunder and hail, and lightning flashed
down to the ground. So the LORD rained hail on the land
of Egypt; hail fell and lightning flashed back and forth.
It was the worst storm in all the land of
Egypt since it had become a nation.
EXODUS 9:23–25

Again God warned Pharaoh of destruction to come, and again the Egyptian ruler ignored Him. So at God's command, heavy, damaging hail fell throughout Egypt, except on His people, the Israelites. It fell on people, animals, and fields, in the worst storm that nation had ever experienced.

As if the fields hadn't had a hard enough time under the plagues, now everything grown in the land was destroyed, even the trees.

Finally Pharaoh seemed to repent and turn to God, but Moses could tell this was not true repentance. Still, Moses prayed that the hail would stop, and it did. As soon as his land was no longer damaged by the storm, Pharaoh again hardened his heart.

Real repentance does not come and go. One who turns to the Lord in faith will not quickly decide it was all a mistake or return to former hard-heartedness. Sure, we all make mistakes, but a heart touched by God will always show.

And the LORD said to Moses,
"Stretch out your hand over Egypt so that locusts
will swarm over the land and devour everything growing
in the fields, everything left by the hail." So Moses stretched out
his staff over Egypt, and the LORD made an east wind blow
across the land all that day and all that night. By morning the
wind had brought the locusts; they invaded all Egypt and settled
down in every area of the country in great numbers. Never
before had there been such a plague of locusts, nor will there
ever be again. They covered all the ground until it was black.
They devoured all that was left after the hail—everything
growing in the fields and the fruit on the trees.
EXODUS 10:12–15

When Moses again appeared at his doorstep, Pharaoh had to know it wasn't with good news. Sure enough, Moses came with another warning: Let my people go to worship, or you will be inundated with locusts.

After Moses left, Pharaoh had a discussion with his officials, who counseled him to let the Israelites go worship. Did he realize Egypt was ruined? they asked.

So Pharaoh unbent a little, called back the prophet and his brother, and said he'd allow the Israelites to worship. But there was one catch: Only the men could go. And of course God would not settle for that! So again Egypt received a plague. An east wind blew over the land and brought with it locusts by the ton. They covered all the land and ate what few green things remained. If the counselors of Pharaoh thought they were ruined before, this was even worse. What few farmers had survived the former plagues were now ruined, too.

Quickly, Pharaoh called back Moses and Aaron and asked them to stop the plague. But again, once the plague was gone, it was as if Egypt's king had forgotten it ever happened.

Pharaoh was a proud man but not one who learned quickly. He seemed unable to realize that a ploy that had not worked before would not work a second time. And he had promised to free the Israelites more than once.

Are we like Pharaoh? When God tells us to do one thing, do we repeatedly try to head in another direction? What are we thinking when we act that way? Does God change His mind or forget what went before? Pharaoh was stubborn in defeat, and it did not work. Neither will it benefit us. Let's obey God the first time instead.

DARKNESS FALLS ON EGYPT

*Then the L*ORD *said to Moses, "Stretch out your hand toward the sky so that darkness will spread over Egypt— darkness that can be felt." So Moses stretched out his hand toward the sky, and total darkness covered all Egypt for three days. No one could see anyone else or leave his place for three days. Yet all the Israelites had light in the places where they lived.*
EXODUS 10:21–23

Without warning Pharaoh, the Lord commanded Moses to begin the ninth plague, and the prophet stretched a hand toward the sky. Darkness spread throughout the land of Egypt. But it was not the normal darkness of night; it was one the people could feel. It was so thick no one could see anyone else, and even the lamps that lit Egyptian homes could not break through it.

The Egyptians would have understood the meaning of this plague, for they worshiped Ra, the sun god. But for three days they could not celebrate the sunrise. God was showing the people that He was more powerful than their pagan deity. So it's not surprising that the Hebrew people still had light.

An irritated Pharaoh called Moses to him and commanded the Hebrews to go worship God, but again he tried to hold on to the slaves, insisting that they leave their flocks behind. Moses pointed out that they could not make sacrifices without the animals. The king's heart hardened again.

Pharaoh commanded Moses never to darken his door again, on pain of death. The prohibition seems to have been fine with the prophet. By now the two men were probably tired of seeing each other in this spiritual and political deadlock.

Those who are blinded by unbelief live in darkness as black as the ninth plague. As Christians, who enjoy the benefits of the Light, we often wonder why people will not turn to Him. Their darkness is not the ordinary middle-of-the-night sort, but one that so thoroughly covers the eyes that they have no inkling of the Light.

What lifts this darkness? Only repentance and faith in Jesus. We can discuss faith with unbelievers until we turn blue in the face, but until they trust in Him, they cannot fully understand.

DEATH OF THE FIRSTBORN

*At midnight the LORD struck down all the firstborn
in Egypt, from the firstborn of Pharaoh, who sat on the throne,
to the firstborn of the prisoner, who was in the dungeon,
and the firstborn of all the livestock as well. Pharaoh and all his
officials and all the Egyptians got up during the night, and there
was loud wailing in Egypt, for there was not a house without
someone dead. During the night Pharaoh summoned Moses
and Aaron and said, "Up! Leave my people, you and the
Israelites! Go, worship the LORD as you have requested."*
EXODUS 12:29–31

Without warning to anyone but the Hebrews, God acted. Moses and all His people had received God's directions for celebrating the Passover. Every household would put lamb's blood on the doorposts and lintel. The lamb would be roasted for dinner, and they would eat it with unleavened bread and bitter herbs. All the people were to be dressed for travel and ready to leave as soon as the order came. As they hurriedly obeyed all God's directions, the Israelites must have had a sense of intense excitement running through their community. God was going to do something spectacular!

The death of the firstborn Egyptian in each family came as a shock to Egypt's leaders. In the middle of the night, Pharaoh lost his son, but the plague did not end there, nor did the ruler immediately declare that God's people could leave. Every Egyptian household, even the humblest, lost the oldest child, and none remained unaffected. Even the livestock lost their firstborn. The wailing in Egypt must have been awful to hear. But the Hebrews, off east in Goshen, wouldn't have heard it.

Finally, after this sudden affliction, Pharaoh understood he was vanquished and called back the man he'd declared he'd never see alive. When Moses came, the ruler agreed to let all the Hebrews, with every one of their flocks and herds, go. It was a terrible comedown for the leader of a world power.

Egypt's populace couldn't see the backs of the Israelites quickly enough. The people of this wealthy land gave the former slaves gold, silver, and clothing, hoping they'd leave before every Egyptian died. That's how God prepared His people for their long journey.

The Israelites, standing ready, grabbed their unleavened dough and carried it with them. They hurried off before Pharaoh could change his mind.

While the Egyptians had been punished through the ten plagues, God had blessed His own people. They had remained untouched by the plague horrors, and now they received physical benefits from the people who had enslaved them. The Egyptian goods would provide for God's people as they traveled through the desert. And they would need all of it, since their trip would last many years.

Because of their rebellion against Him, God inflicted great pain on the Egyptians. Though He'd made it clear He was more powerful than their own gods, they preferred to stick with their familiar deities and live in sin. So they brought their troubles on themselves.

But the unwitting Israelites did not take this warning God placed before them, either. On the trip into the Promised Land, they began to doubt the Lord who delivered them. As they faced hardship, they doubted His care for them. For their rebellion against God, they spent forty years in the wilderness between Egypt and the Promised Land.

Are we tempted to doubt? Let's remember both the Egyptians and Israelites and take heart again. Trusting God will never be a bad choice.

*Then Moses stretched out his hand over the sea; and the LORD
caused the sea to go back by a strong east wind all that night,
and made the sea into dry land, and the waters were divided.
So the children of Israel went into the midst of the sea on
the dry ground, and the waters were a wall to them
on their right hand and on their left.*
EXODUS 14:21–22 NKJV

After the tenth and final plague, when Pharaoh allowed them
to leave Egypt, the Israelites hurried off into the desert. But
instead of worshiping God by making burnt offerings, they
worshiped with their feet—obedient to God, they set off to
the Promised Land and freedom from bondage!

Pharaoh heard his slaves were not returning, called out
his chariot force, and headed after them. It could hardly have
been a surprise to him that they did as he'd expected them to
do and headed for the hills.

The Israelites looked up and saw the Egyptian forces
following them, and terror filled their hearts. First they cried
out to God; then they began to blame Moses for leading
them into the desert to die. "Weren't there enough graves in
Egypt?" they demanded. "Why did you bring us here when
we told you to leave us alone?" Their hindsight wasn't exactly
20/20, was it? They'd been happy enough to leave Egypt.

God, knowing they might run back to Pharaoh's land in
such circumstances, had backed them up against the Red Sea.

They had nowhere to go, so Moses ordered them to stand firm in God, who would deliver them. "The Lord will fight for you," he promised.

God directed Moses and his people to move forward as the prophet held out his hand over the sea, and He promised that the waters would divide before them. The angel of the Lord, who had gone before them, turned and stood behind God's people, and the cloud of God's presence joined him as a rearguard.

Moses stretched out one hand, and through the night the sea was driven back by a strong east wind. The waters separated into two walls, and dry land appeared between them. The Israelites and all their animals walked dry-shod between the two walls of water.

After the Israelites entered the sea, the Egyptians dashed after them. At the end of this long night, God threw the opponents of His people into confusion. Their chariot wheels began to fall off their vehicles, and their destruction was imminent. By now the Egyptians were experienced enough to know why this was happening. "Let's get away," they cried. "God is fighting for the Israelites" (see 14:25). They knew the Lord's power and feared Him but still would not bow the knee to this mighty One who had outdone their own idols.

God commanded Moses to raise his hand again, and the water closed over the Egyptian warriors. They were swept off into the sea, and none survived. According to Moses' praise song after this event, Pharaoh lost the best of his officers (see 15:4).

But all the Israelites had passed safely through the sea.

As Moses had prophesied, they would never again see any of those Egyptians. On dry land again, Israel had a praise party, worshiping the Lord who had saved them from their enslavers.

Moses had commanded his people to stand firm and watch God fight for them, and they had seen Him do just that as the waters enveloped their pursuers. God has not stopped fighting for His people. He still protects them from their enemies and watches their backs.

If the Israelites could trust Him when their backs were to the sea, can we do any less? No matter what we face today, if we've trusted in Him, we are His children. He will never fail us. What enemy need we fear?

MOSES MALIGNED

*And the people thirsted there for water, and the people
complained against Moses, and said, "Why is it you have
brought us up out of Egypt, to kill us and our children and our
livestock with thirst?" So Moses cried out to the LORD, saying,
"What shall I do with this people? They are almost ready to stone
me!" And the LORD said to Moses, "Go on before the people, and
take with you some of the elders of Israel. Also take in your hand
your rod with which you struck the river, and go. Behold,
I will stand before you there on the rock in Horeb; and
you shall strike the rock, and water will come out
of it, that the people may drink."*

EXODUS 17:3–6 NKJV

As the Israelites traveled toward their new home, they became
distinctly crabby. It wasn't the easiest journey, and at times it
must have seemed to Moses that every one of the millions
of people he was escorting had something to say about the
difficulties of the trip. It didn't matter that God turned bitter
water sweet at Marah or sent manna and quail to feed His
hungry people. The Israelites, looking back at their lives in
Egypt, wanted something better. Every time they faced a
challenge, they acted as if they were about to die.

Moses feared his own people would take his life. They'd
given him an ultimatum: Either he gave them water, or they
would stone him as a traitor! So the prophet consulted with
God. The Lord told Moses to take with him some elders and

the staff with which he'd struck the Nile. God promised to stand before him at Horeb. As the prophet struck the rock, water would flow out.

The people wanted a judgment, and God gave them one, with their elders as witnesses. But the judgment was not on His prophet. God stood before the people and protected Moses, who had done His will faithfully, despite the Israelites' grumbling.

If we seek to criticize one of God's faithful leaders, we'd best beware. For God does not take such actions lightly. When we follow a leader who walks closely with God, it's better to appreciate him than grumble. Was God planning on letting His people die of thirst in the desert on their way to the Promised Land? That's unthinkable—except to those complaining Israelites. Had they trusted, they would have both received water and failed to malign Moses.

Are we grumbling Israelites?

THE LOST REBELLION

*Now it came to pass, as he finished speaking all these words,
that the ground split apart under them, and the earth
opened its mouth and swallowed them up, with their house-
holds and all the men with Korah, with all their goods.
So they and all those with them went down alive
into the pit; the earth closed over them, and they
perished from among the assembly.*

NUMBERS 16:31–33 NKJV

On what probably seemed an ordinary day as he went about his work as a prophet, Moses suddenly faced rebellion in the ranks of the Israelites.

The prophet had simply commanded them to wear tassels on their robes to remind them to be holy to God. In response, two groups of malcontents forged an agreement and rose up against him. Dathan, Abiram, and On of the Reubenites might not have been a surprise, but Korah was a Levite, one of Moses and Aaron's tribe, a man who served in the tabernacle. With these four stood 250 congregational leaders.

It was hardly a disagreement over tassels. The insurgents claimed all the people in the congregation were holy—a manifestly ridiculous statement, assuming that every one of millions of people was without sin. More than likely, these proud rebels felt guilty about their own sins and sought to cover them up with noisy complaints. Then they accused Moses and Aaron of exalting themselves above the rest of Israel.

Moses didn't argue—he reproved Korah for his dissatisfaction with his temple role, then simply allowed God to judge. He called everyone to come to the tabernacle the next day, but the rebellious Reubenites refused the invitation.

The following day, the rest assembled, censers in hand, at the tent of meeting. God warned Aaron and Moses to step away from the rebels, and the two men quickly fell before God in prayer. In response to their plea for their people, the Lord told them to warn the innocent ones to stay far from the errant Reubenites who stood at the openings of their tents watching the events before them.

Moses described the terms of God's judgment: The Lord would destroy those who had sinned by swallowing them up in the earth. Immediately the ground split and gobbled up Korah and the rebel Reubenites. Fire destroyed their 250 supporters. All the rest of Israel fled, fearing God's wrath on themselves.

Here, God gives us a concrete picture of what He thinks of rebellion against Him. For rebellion against His appointed, faithful leaders can also be rebellion against the Lord they serve.

Have we been tempted to rebel against God by attacking His devoted followers, especially those leading in His name? Maybe we'd best watch the ground beneath us!

SPARE THE ROD?

*And Moses spake unto the children of Israel, and every one
of their princes gave him a rod apiece, for each prince one,
according to their fathers' houses, even twelve rods: and the
rod of Aaron was among their rods. And Moses laid up the rods
before the LORD in the tabernacle of witness. And it came to
pass, that on the morrow Moses went into the tabernacle
of witness; and, behold, the rod of Aaron for the house
of Levi was budded, and brought forth buds,
and bloomed blossoms, and yielded almonds.*

NUMBERS 17:6–8 KJV

Korah's rebellion didn't end the Israelites' dissatisfaction with
their leaders. Again they rebelled, and Moses' intercession
saved their lives from a plague, but not before 14,700 died.

God chose to end the rebellion with a miracle that
showed everyone whom He wanted in control. At God's
command, the leaders of each one of the twelve tribes of
Israel gave his staff to Moses. In case there was any question,
scripture records that as high priest, Aaron's staff stood for
the tribe of Levi. Each rod had the name of its owner writ-
ten on it, and they were laid before the ark, in the holiest
part of the tabernacle.

The next day, of all the staves, only Aaron's had budded,
bloomed, and fruited with almonds. There was no question
about whose rod it was, since his name was right there for all
to see.

With this concrete proof, the Israelites could have assurance that they were following the right man. God did not spare the rod when it came to letting His people know they had displeased Him. Through a miracle, He set them on the right path again, though, unhappily, it did not completely quell the complaints of His people.

God does not spare the rod when His people fail Him. Sometimes He punishes them, as He did when the plague appeared. But He had a choice: He could wipe out all the rebels, and only a small band of people would reach the Promised Land, or He could show compassion and turn at least some hearts. God chose to be compassionate.

Do we willingly turn to God's will, or does He need to take out a rod and show us what He means? If we demand proof of Him, let's remember that God could spare the rod and send us a death-dealing illness. Do we really want to take that risk?

Doesn't obedience sound a lot more pleasant now?

SNAKE ON A POLE

Therefore the people came to Moses,
and said, We have sinned, for we have spoken against the
LORD, and against thee; pray unto the LORD, that he take away
the serpents from us. And Moses prayed for the people. And the
LORD said unto Moses, Make thee a fiery serpent, and set it upon
a pole: and it shall come to pass, that every one that is bitten,
when he looketh upon it, shall live. And Moses made a
serpent of brass, and put it upon a pole, and it came to pass,
that if a serpent had bitten any man, when he
beheld the serpent of brass, he lived.

NUMBERS 21:7–9 KJV

The Israelites had a nationwide attitude problem. No matter what Moses and Aaron said or what miracle God showed them, they were determined that life was miserable and they had to have things their way. Now Aaron was dead, and ignoring the fact that God had just given them victory over the king of Arad, again they began to grumble.

"Why did you bring us into the wilderness?" they whined at Moses in their familiar chorus. "We're tired of manna today, manna tomorrow, and manna for who knows how long." They even called the manna "worthless."

Had they forgotten their hunger in the desert, when they first began the trip to the Promised Land? These determinedly sinful people seemingly forgot how painful their slavery had been and looked back longingly to Egypt. Did they remember how difficult it had been to make strawless bricks?

So began a real whinefest, for they not only complained about Moses, but having lost the convenient target of Aaron, they complained about the Lord, too. Did they simply like complaining because it gave them an opportunity to hear their own voices? Well, no one else wanted to hear it—especially not God. What were they thinking, to expect that He would put up with their petty complaints? Past experience should have made them wiser. God didn't ignore their whining and complaining. Instead, He sent a fearsome affliction: fiery, poisonous serpents that bit the people. Many Israelites died.

Now they remembered their previous experiences, and the remaining sinners knew where to go when they were in trouble. The suddenly penitent people knocked on the flap of Moses' tent, seeking salvation. They asked Moses to pray, and the prophet immediately responded to their need.

God heard the prayers of His prophet and provided a way for their physical salvation: He commanded Moses to make a snake and set it on a pole, and those who were bitten could look at it and live. This miracle turned around the effect of the fearsome plague of snakes and showed forth God's abundant compassion on His failure-prone people.

Obediently, Moses fashioned a bronze serpent and set it on a pole. Those who looked upon it would not die, even though they had been bitten. How many Israelites would have been foolish enough to refuse that sight? Only those so steeped in sin and foolish that they had no fear of God or the poisonous snakes.

It's not hard to understand why theologians see Jesus in this Old Testament image. For we, too, look upward to a kind of pole for our salvation. In the cross is our only hope, since none of us have failed to bellyache when we have not liked the direction in which God has sent us. Or, if we've avoided that sin, we've looked back to our own Egypt, the site of our previous sin-filled life. None of us fails to be affected by moral and spiritual failure, so all of us need to look to the cross for our salvation. It will not stop sin from biting us, but it will bring us to the gracious Father, through the sacrifice of His only Son.

THE RED SEA REVISTED

*The priests who carried the ark of the covenant of the LORD
stood firm on dry ground in the middle of the Jordan,
while all Israel passed by until the whole nation had
completed the crossing on dry ground.*

JOSHUA 3:17

It took Israel two tries to cross the Jordan River. Forty
years earlier spies had doubted that Israel could conquer,
and that doubt had condemned a generation to wander
in the desert for forty years. This time the men sent into
Jericho gave a good report. So Israel prepared to enter
Canaan.

None of the people who stood on the bank of the river
had been there before. But the new generation joyfully
consecrated themselves to enter the new land. Ready for
success, they trusted God.

The priests carried the ark of the covenant forward, into
the flow of the river, and the stream of water stopped, just as
it had at the Red Sea when Moses led Israel out of Egypt.
When everyone reached the other side, dry-shod, God commanded that they leave a memorial of twelve stones in the
river.

Like the second-generation Israelites, do we have memo-
rials to the work God has done in our lives? Do we remain
mindful of His blessings and power? Let's not make God

turn us away from blessings because we've doubted. We don't want to miss out on the best things He has planned for our lives!

TUMBLING WALLS

On the seventh day they rose early, at the dawn of day, and marched around the city in the same manner seven times. . . . And at the seventh time, when the priests had blown the trumpets, Joshua said to the people, "Shout, for the LORD has given you the city." . . . So the people shouted, and the trumpets were blown. As soon as the people heard the sound of the trumpet, the people shouted a great shout, and the wall fell down flat.
JOSHUA 6:15–16, 20 ESV

When God commanded the Israelites to head for Jericho, it must have been an intimidating prospect. This was the oldest walled city in the world; a strategically placed trade metropolis. The Lord had an admirable battle plan when He directed the attack of these walls that defended the Palestinian hill country. But when the Israelites first set eyes on Jericho, they could have feared that success was likely to come at a high price. Yet they took heart in the fact that God promised that the city was already theirs, for He had given it into their hands.

With God in command of this expedition, it was about to be a battle unlike any other. When Israel headed for the city, the people of Jericho shut themselves behind the walls and probably hoped that the Israelite army would pass them by. As God's army camped outside their walls, the city dwellers must have become terribly confused. For the newcomers did not attack. Instead, an army of silent Israelites surrounded seven priests with their constantly blaring ram's horn trumpets and marched around the city once a day for six days. Each time, following their walk around Jericho, the men returned to their camp. By the end of the third day, everyone inside the walls must have been jittery. What could this mean?

On the seventh day, when nerves on both sides may have been tight, God commanded His army to march around the city seven times. The Israelites rose early to get at the job. Can you see the people standing on Jericho's walls, counting? One, two, three, four. . .

After the Israelites had silently circumnavigated the city six times and were ending their final round, Joshua told his men to shout, for God had given them the city. As they shouted, the walls of the city fell down flat. So the Israelites went into the city and captured it.

God had commanded Joshua that everything in the city was to be destroyed—all the people and animals. The only human exceptions were Rahab's family. Since this woman of Jericho had hidden the Israelite spies who scoped out the situation in her city, God preserved her and her household. And all the valuable vessels in the city were gathered to be made part of the Lord's treasury.

Though archaeologists have disagreed over the dating of the destruction of the Old Testament city of Jericho, there is clear evidence that it was completely destroyed. Actually, there were two walls around the city, one six feet thick and an inner one, twelve feet thick. In a 1930 archaeological report, the outer wall is described as having fallen down the slope of the hill. The inner wall remained standing only near the citadel. The rest of the city had been destroyed by fire, and some evidence shows this occurred suddenly.

If we spend much time arguing about archaeological issues that may never be proved either way, will we miss the point of this story? God performed this miracle in order to bring His people into the Promised Land. He devised a battle plan that took few if any Israelite lives and eradicated a pagan people whose pagan practices could have quickly destroyed the faith of His own people.

But God did not simply tumble down walls then forget about His people in the following centuries. The walls He destroys today may not be physical ones, but He still removes dangers that lure believers from truth and keep them from fulfilling His mission.

What wall has tumbled down before you?

Then Joshua spoke to the LORD in the day when the LORD
delivered up the Amorites before the children of Israel, and he
said in the sight of Israel: "Sun, stand still over Gibeon; and
Moon, in the Valley of Aijalon." So the sun stood still, and the
moon stopped, till the people had revenge upon their enemies. . . .
So the sun stood still in the midst of heaven, and did not hasten
to go down for about a whole day. And there has been no
day like that, before it or after it, that the LORD heeded
the voice of a man; for the LORD fought for Israel.
JOSHUA 10:12–14 NKJV

When Adoni-zedek, king of Jerusalem, heard that Israel had captured the city of Ai and that the great city of Gibeon, only six miles from his city, had made peace with the invaders, he was filled with fear. What would this strange people, who had quickly conquered other cities in Canaan, do to his city? *Better to attack one of Israel's friends and fight on our own terms than wait for these Israeli invaders to come to us,* he must have thought. *After all, look what happened to Jericho.*

So Jerusalem's king sent a message to the other Amorite kings of the city-states of southern Canaan and invited them to unite with him on a military campaign against Gibeon. Five kings banded together to take on a single peaceful city: Hoham, king of Hebron; Piram, king of Jarmuth; Japhia, king of Lachish; and Debir, king of Eglon, joined their armies to

Adoni-zedek's and headed for Gibeon.

One day Gibeon peacefully sat in the sun, the next they saw an army on the horizon. Before they closed their gates, Gibeon's citizens sent a message to Joshua, encamped with his people in Gilgal. Their short missive could be translated in a single word: "Help!"

Though Gibeon had tricked Israel into making the treaty with them, Joshua did not fail the city. God promised that the gathered armies would not stand before his army, so Israel's leader confidently headed out with his warriors. After marching all night, traveling about twenty miles uphill, the Israeli army attacked the Amorites. Struck by the Lord with a sense of panic, the Canaanite attackers fled before Joshua's troops. Israel got a new burst of energy and chased the enemy for miles, cutting soldiers down as they ran. As the Amorites dashed away from Beth Horon, God rained large hailstones down on the enemy. More men died at God's hand of judgment than at the hands of His people.

As the day waned, in an unusual prayer, Joshua asked God to make the sun and moon to stand still while Israel avenged themselves on their enemies. Some scholars believe it was a request for a longer day in which to finish the battle.

God's people were victorious and extended their control of Canaan through this battle. Only a remnant of the warriors escaped into fortified cities. As Israel chased the Amorites, their terrified kings hid in a cave. Joshua decreed his men should block the five rulers in their safe place until the battle was finished. Following the end of the engagement, Joshua killed all five as a sign of the Lord's judgment on Israel's enemies.

As a by-product of the battle with the Amorite kings, Makkedah, one of the cities in the path of the running battle, was also conquered by Israel and completely destroyed. Six kings conquered in one day has to be some kind of record! One that could be accomplished only with God's power.

Scripture comments that there was never a day like that one, when God listened to the voice of man. And it's true that God does not often stop the sun and moon in their courses. But He does listen to prayer every day. So if we face attackers from five different places, we need not fear. God answers prayer—sometimes in amazing ways. But we do need to pray.

ONE WEAK SPOT

Behold, a young lion roared against [Samson].
And the Spirit of the LORD came mightily upon him,
and he rent him as he would have rent a kid, and he had
nothing in his hand. . . . And the Spirit of the LORD came
upon him, and he went down to Ashkelon, and slew
thirty men of them, and took their spoil.
JUDGES 14:5–6, 19 KJV

No wine or strong drink should have passed Nazarite Samson's lips, so an alcohol abuse problem probably had nothing to do with his sudden desire to show off his muscles. Scripture tells us that the power of God's Spirit gave him a strength that must have amazed the elders of his day and made the young men pick up their weights and pray that God would so bless them. But no one was as powerful as the Bible's strong man. When the men of Gaza wanted to kill him, Samson took a midnight stroll, grabbed the city gates, and carried them off to Hebron (see 16:3).

But the strong man had one weak spot: women. He could never keep a secret from one. When Samson became entangled with the beautiful Delilah, Israel's Philistine overlords came to her and demanded that she seduce Samson and discover the secret of his strength. They'd pay her well. She nagged at her lover, and three times he lied to her. Finally, he dropped his guard and told her that if she shaved his head, he would become weak. When Delilah had a man shave him, Samson lost his power—probably more because he'd repeatedly contravened his Nazarite vows than because he lost his hair.

The Philistines blinded Samson and made him a slave, but when his hair grew, he regained his strength. During a pagan Philistine festival, the Philistines demanded that Samson entertain them. Following his performance, the Israelite did his best act: He pushed down two of the weight-bearing pillars in the temple, destroying the building and all the people in it.

Samson proves that even the strongest man has weaknesses. Though he had astonishing physical prowess, Samson's moral and spiritual powers were slowly depleted as he broke the vows that set him apart to be holy to the Lord. Let's take Samson's example to heart and keep ourselves daily devoted to God. For Samson's failings did not happen quickly: He slowly slipped into error as he forgot his vows and the commandments God had given His people.

*"I will call upon the LORD to send thunder and rain.
And you will realize what an evil thing you did in the eyes of
the LORD when you asked for a king." Then Samuel called upon
the LORD, and that same day the LORD sent thunder and rain.
So all the people stood in awe of the LORD and of Samuel.*

1 SAMUEL 12:17–18

In his last address to his people, Samuel pled with his rebellious people, who had denied God by asking for a king, to be faithful to their Lord. If they obeyed King Saul and did right, all would be well, he promised.

To prove that his words were not simply idle chatter and that God was Lord, the prophet told Israel to watch. Then he called on God to send thunder and rain. Though it was the dry season, the thunder crashed and the rain plummeted from the skies. Impressed and understanding their own sinfulness and God's power, the Israelites suddenly feared they might die.

It wasn't as if Samuel had never before told the people about sin. They'd heard his words but never accepted them, but his miracle finally stopped them in their tracks and made them realize what they'd done.

Has God spoken to us of sin, and we've tried to ignore it? Does He have to jounce us out of our complacency with a notification that He's still in control?

RAINMAKER

*Now Elijah the Tishbite, from Tishbe in Gilead, said to Ahab,
"As the LORD, the God of Israel, lives, whom I serve,
there will be neither dew nor rain in the next
few years except at my word."*
1 KINGS 17:1

Israel's King Ahab was one in a long line of disobedient kings. But his forebears couldn't hold a candle to this evil ruler. Through the influence of his wife, Jezebel, he served the pagan god Baal and fell into exceedingly wicked ways.

So the Lord sent the prophet Elijah to the king with a message: Unless Elijah gave the word, no rain or even dew would fall on the nation. Then God had the prophet hide by a brook east of the Jordan. When that stream dried up, God sent the prophet away from Israel, to Zarephath in Sidon.

After three years of drought, God sent Elijah back to parched Israel and her king. Elijah had a showdown with the priests of Baal that proved their god Baal impotent. After the pagan priests were killed, Elijah prayed for rain, and it poured down on Israel, proving that the Lord, not Baal, controlled the weather—and everything else, too.

Over and over, God uses His control of this world to show forth His power. Are we open to that message? Or will it take a three-year drought to get our attention?

SOME OIL AND FLOUR

The widow answered, "In the name of the living LORD your God, I swear that I don't have any bread. All I have is a handful of flour and a little olive oil. I'm on my way home now with these few sticks to cook what I have for my son and me. After that, we will starve to death." Elijah said, "Everything will be fine. Do what you said. Go home and fix something for you and your son. But first, please make a small piece of bread and bring it to me. The LORD God of Israel has promised that your jar of flour won't run out and your bottle of oil won't dry up before he sends rain for the crops."
1 KINGS 17:12–14 CEV

Elijah hadn't been living well while he hid from Ahab in the Kerith Ravine, though he had water and food, since ravens miraculously delivered his meals. But the stream that provided the water dried up, and the prophet had to move on.

God told the thirsty prophet to head for Zarephath of Sidon, a small seaside town. It seemed an odd place for God to send him. After all, the Phoenicians were Gentiles who worshiped Baal, the pagan god whose worship had infiltrated Israel. And Queen Jezebel, who had brought such worship into Israel, hated Elijah. Though there seemed to be no sense in the place God had sent His prophet, in going there, Elijah became the first prophet to reach out to the Gentiles.

Not only did God send His prophet into Baal country,

He sent him to a very poor widow. For widows of that age, poverty was common. They had no career paths open to them, and unless a family member took care of them, they could easily end up destitute. That's the situation this woman found herself in. She was gathering firewood, about to make a last meal for herself and her son. There was nothing more in the cupboard, and she did not expect to have anything in the future.

So when Elijah asked for some water and food, the woman willingly went for his drink but was not enthusiastic about sharing the little food she had. She explained her situation to the prophet, who told her it would be all right: her flour and oil would not run out before the rain came.

Perhaps this woman had no faith in the Lord God, but with deference she referred to Him as "the living LORD your God" (17:12 CEV). She trustingly followed the prophet's directions, and everything happened as Elijah promised. For many days, they had enough to eat, even if it wasn't a perfectly balanced diet.

God provided for the widow, her son, and the prophet, when her own god failed her. He even provided for these three while His own people suffered from the drought. Surely she must have thought about the power of a God who did this. Perhaps she even came to know Him because of it.

Had the people of Israel known where Elijah was, they probably would have thrown a fit. Why was he living in this pagan village instead of providing them with the water they needed? They might have been dumbfounded at the idea that this unbeliever was cared for while they struggled so.

But God had a twofold purpose: The Israelites would learn of their own sinfulness while He saved the life of this poor widow.

God does not see people the way we do. To us, well-to-do, powerful, or highly spiritual people seem important. We can imagine God doing wonderful things for them. But so often, God chooses to bless the quietly faithful or totally unworldly person we'd pass by in a minute.

Sometimes we stand amazed when good things happen to unbelievers and wonder why the faithful Christian is passed over. We need to understand that God has His own purposes. He's working out a wider plan that may bring salvation to a hurting soul. Let's not judge too quickly. Instead, let's trust in the Lord who rules this earth and can touch any heart in it.

*Then [Elijah] cried out to the LORD and said, "O LORD my God,
have You also brought tragedy on the widow with whom I lodge,
by killing her son?" And he stretched himself out on the child
three times, and cried out to the LORD and said, "O LORD
my God, I pray, let this child's soul come back to him."
Then the LORD heard the voice of Elijah; and the soul
of the child came back to him, and he revived.*

1 KINGS 17:20–22 NKJV

One day, the widow with whom Elijah was lodging in
Zarephath came to him, lamenting. Was he trying to make
her aware of her own sin, she asked, by taking the life of her
only son? For the boy, her only hope in old age, had become
terribly ill and now was not breathing. The grieving mother
had begun to wonder if she'd done wrong in taking in the
prophet who stood before her.

Elijah didn't stop to ask why she hadn't consulted him
earlier. He picked up her son, took him to his own room, and
laid him on the bed. Stretching out on the boy, he prayed
fervently, crying out to God, almost repeating the widow's
words to him. He pointed out to God the benefit this woman
had been to him, opening her home to him.

Obviously, in the time he'd been there, Elijah had come
to care for this little family. The fact that they were Sidonians,
not Israelites, did not matter. The widow had taken Elijah
in though she and her son were in desperate straits, and he

valued her for her deep-pocketed kindness.

The Lord heard the prophet's prayer, and the boy miraculously regained his life—the first time such a thing had ever happened. Elijah picked up the boy and returned him to his mother. What joy must have filled them when they saw the work God had done.

The widow, convinced that Elijah was just what he said he was, declared: "Now by this I know that you are a man of God, and that the word of the LORD in your mouth *is* the truth" (17:24 NKJV). Can one doubt that by this point she had come to faith?

God's compassion on the widow is such a touching story. But is He any less tender to His people today? Those who call on Him in pain will know His gentle love.

"O Lord, God of Abraham, Isaac, and Israel, let it be known this day that you are God in Israel, and that I am your servant, and that I have done all these things at your word. Answer me, O Lord, answer me, that this people may know that you, O Lord, are God, and that you have turned their hearts back."
Then the fire of the Lord fell and consumed the burnt offering and the wood and the stones and the dust, and licked up the water that was in the trench.
1 Kings 18:36–38 ESV

As Elijah entered Israel and met the king, Ahab greeted him with the words, "Is it you, you troubler of Israel?" (18:17 ESV). Nice to have been greeted so warmly, wasn't it, when he controlled the rain flow over the nation! Three years of drought surely hadn't improved Ahab's disposition or gotten God's message through to him.

Elijah told the king to bring together all the pagan priests and prophets whom Jezebel supported at Israel's expense. Perhaps because he wanted to end the drought, the king obeyed. They met Elijah and all Israel's people on Mount Carmel. There Elijah confronted the Israelites about their idolatry and proposed a simple showdown: The priests of Baal would make one offering, and Elijah would make another. The one whose sacrifice was consumed by fire would be the better deity.

The people liked that idea. So the priests of Baal prepared

their offering and called on Baal for half a day. At noon, Elijah mocked their god and the stories their religion told of this anthropomorphic deity. Desperate, worshipers began mutilating themselves to try to get Baal's attention, but of course it did not work. Now it was Elijah's turn.

After calling his people to himself, Elijah took twelve stones, symbolic of each of Israel's tribes, and rebuilt the Lord's altar, which had been destroyed by the idolaters. The prophet made a trench around the altar that would have held about fourteen quarts of seeds. Then he set the wood on the altar and cut up the sacrificial bull. He had some men fill four jars with water and pour it over the offering and wood. They did this three times, until water ran round the altar and filled the trench.

Then Elijah prayed: "O LORD, God of Abraham, Isaac, and Israel, let it be known this day that you are God in Israel, and that I am your servant, and that I have done all these things at your word. Answer me, O LORD, answer me, that this people may know that you, O LORD, are God, and that you have turned their hearts back" (verses 36–37 ESV). No ranting and raving, no cutting himself. Just a simple prayer.

The fire of the Lord fell and miraculously consumed the offering, the water, the wood, stones, and dust, and licked up the water in the trench. The Baal worshipers had no chance to imply that there'd been any funny business going on.

When they saw this sign of wonder, the people fell on their faces and started repeating, "The LORD, he is God" over and over (verse 39). They'd gotten the point. While their faith was strong, Elijah commanded them to grab Baal's priests.

They did, and all the pagan priests were slaughtered in the Kishon Valley (verse 40).

Elijah prophesied that a heavy rain was coming and went to the top of the mountain to pray that God would end this curse on His people. After repeated checks on the sky, his servant reported a small cloud on the horizon. Shortly dark clouds appeared, and the rain poured down. God's drought was at an end.

"How long will you waver?" Elijah asked his people when he confronted them about their idolatry (see verse 21). They had gone back and forth between pagan beliefs and knowledge of the Lord. Now the prophet showed them clearly who to believe in.

Are we tempted to waver? Let's remember the power God showed on that day and turn back to Him. He strengthens His people when they trust in Him.

JUDGMENT BY FIRE

*The captain went up to Elijah, who was sitting on the top of
a hill, and said to him, "Man of God, the king says, 'Come
down!'" Elijah answered the captain, "If I am a man of God,
may fire come down from heaven and consume you
and your fifty men!" Then fire fell from heaven
and consumed the captain and his men.*

2 KINGS 1:9–10

Israel's King Ahaziah succeeded his father, Ahab, and walked
in his wicked footsteps. When Ahaziah injured himself in an
accident, he sent to inquire of Baal-Zebub, Ekron's god, if he
would be healed.

God sent Elijah to the king's messengers to ask if Israel
had no God and to tell them the king would die. When the
men returned to Ahaziah, the king sent a captain and fifty
men to the prophet to call him to himself. But Elijah called
down fire from heaven, and all fifty-one were consumed. The
stubborn king sent another company of men to the prophet,
and they met the same end (verses 10–12).

The third captain was wiser and begged Elijah to have
compassion. So God allowed Elijah to go to the king. Not
that it changed the message. Elijah repeated what he'd said
before, and the king died (verses 13–17).

Sometimes we ignore the tenderheartedness of God. Do
we know that we can hurt Him when we go elsewhere with
our troubles? What problem should we bring to Him today?

*Elijah took his cloak, rolled it up and struck the
water with it. The water divided to the right and to the left,
and the two of them crossed over on dry ground. . . .
[Elisha] picked up the cloak that had fallen from Elijah
and went back and stood on the bank of the Jordan. Then he took
the cloak that had fallen from him and struck the water with it.
"Where now is the LORD, the God of Elijah?" he asked.
When he struck the water, it divided to the right
and to the left, and he crossed over.*

2 KINGS 2:8, 13–14

Elijah wasn't telling him about it, but his disciple Elisha knew God planned to take his master to heaven, and he wasn't going to miss that. He followed Elijah the whole day. When they went to cross the Jordan, Elijah rolled up his cloak like a staff and struck the water with it. Like Joshua, the prophet and his disciple saw the Jordan divide, and they walked through on dry ground.

On the other side of the Jordan, chariots of fire appeared, and Elijah went to God on a whirlwind. Then the sorrowing disciple took up Elijah's cloak and repeated his miracle, proving himself Elijah's successor.

Want to know if people are what they claim? Look at their lives. What they do proves who they are, just as Elisha's miracle showed others that God had given him His power.

SPRING RENEWAL

*Then he went out to the spring and threw the salt into it, saying,
"This is what the LORD says: 'I have healed this water. Never
again will it cause death or make the land unproductive.' "
And the water has remained wholesome to this day,
according to the word Elisha had spoken.*

2 KINGS 2:21–22

After Elisha took on the mantle of his teacher, the men of
Jericho came to him with a problem: Their water was bad.
The new prophet asked for a bowl of salt. He took it to their
spring, tossed in the salt, and the water was healed.

Much of Elisha's ministry focuses on compassionate,
personal miracles, so it's appropriate that it should begin so.
Obviously, salt alone would not have made their water more
potable, but it was also a sign of God's covenant with His
people. The Lord improved the water that sustained their
lives.

When God does good things for us, do we recognize that
He's keeping covenant with us? Are we keeping up our part
of the covenant, too?

NAME-CALLING PUNISHMENT

From there Elisha went up to Bethel.
As he was walking along the road, some youths came
out of the town and jeered at him. "Go on up, you baldhead!"
they said. "Go on up, you baldhead!" He turned around,
looked at them and called down a curse on them in the name
of the LORD. Then two bears came out of the woods
and mauled forty-two of the youths.
2 KINGS 2:23–24

Judgment follows compassion as Elisha curses a horde of youths who jeer at him in Bethel. This city had become the center of idolatry under Jeroboam. Obviously, this crowd of youngsters had picked up all the worst religious habits of their elders. Since forty-two were mauled, it was a large group that defamed the prophet, and perhaps the mauling critters stopped them from taking more belligerent action.

It wasn't gentle, innocent children who mocked the prophet. Their punishment may seem sharp, but their lack of faith and respect for God earned it for them, not mere name-calling.

Do we treat God and His servants with respect? Or do we need to look to the woods and see if a bruin is heading our way?

OVERFLOWING BLESSING

Elisha said, "Go around and ask all your neighbors for empty jars. Don't ask for just a few. Then go inside and shut the door behind you and your sons. Pour oil into all the jars, and as each is filled, put it to one side." She left him and afterward shut the door behind her and her sons. They brought the jars to her and she kept pouring.

2 KINGS 4:3–5

Can't you see this woman and her sons running to every neighbor, borrowing crocks, bottles, and bowls? No vessel in the area avoided spending time in her house. Every corner of her home held a bowl or jar.

With the smidgen of oil she had in the house, she began pouring, and the bowls began to fill. As she moved from one vessel to the next, so must her amazement have grown. Her sons kept bringing her more bowls, and the oil kept flowing.

When they ran out of bowls, the oil stopped. But by then this widow had run out of worries. Instead of having her two sons sold as slaves to make good her dead husband's debt, she had oil to sell. Elisha told her there would be enough left over to take care of her family.

When God gives, He does so generously, providing His people's needs—even ours.

BLESSING GONE WRONG?

When Elisha reached the house, there was the boy lying dead on his couch. He went in, shut the door on the two of them and prayed to the LORD. Then he got on the bed and lay upon the boy, mouth to mouth, eyes to eyes, hands to hands. As he stretched himself out upon him, the boy's body grew warm. Elisha turned away and walked back and forth in the room and then got on the bed and stretched out upon him once more.
The boy sneezed seven times and opened his eyes.

2 KINGS 4:32–35

The wealthy Shunammite woman was one of those people for whom good works is a way of life. She surely knew how to use her money wisely and began by feeding Elisha whenever he came to town. Then she suggested to her husband that they build a little room on their roof for the man. Just to make it more convenient, you know. Now Elisha had a place to spend the night, too.

The prophet had probably stopped by a number of times before he decided to do something for her. But like many selfless people, asked what she needed, she replied, "I'm just fine."

So Elisha got to choose a special gift for her: He conferred with his servant, Gehazi, who pointed out she had no child. So the prophet promised the barren woman the joy of having her own child. She doubted, asking him not to lie to her. But the next spring, she bore a son.

For a few years, all was fine as the child grew. But one morning, at harvesttime, as he visited his father in the fields, the boy's head pained him. The father had his men carry his son home, and the boy sat on his mother's lap, being comforted, until he died at noon.

The sorrowful mom laid her son on the prophet's bed, in the room they'd built for him. Shutting the door behind her, she went out to seek the prophet. Not even her husband knew what had happened.

The Shunammite hurried to Mount Carmel. Before she got to Elisha, the prophet sent Gehazi out to see if all was well. The prophet didn't need a spyglass to know something was up, and it wasn't good. But she would not tell her troubles to any but Elisha. She came to him and grabbed his feet, a sign of respect. Then she started talking. Hadn't he given her a son on his own, without her asking for him? Hadn't she asked him not to deceive her? She was probably thinking it would have been easier never to have had a child than to lose this much-loved boy. How would her heart ever heal?

Elisha tried healing the boy at a distance, sending his servant to the boy with his own staff. Gehazi was to hurry to the Shunammite's home, without speaking to anyone, and lay the staff on the boy's face. But the child remained inert. So the prophet went into the home himself.

Then Elisha did as Elijah had done with the son of the woman of Zarephath. He lay on him, stretching out on the boy, who began to become warm. The prophet walked around a bit, then repeated his previous actions. Suddenly the child sneezed seven times, and what a blessed sound it must have been to his mother. Elisha called his servant and told him to bring her to him. When she saw that her son lived, she fell at the prophet's feet in thanks.

Can we trust God with our most treasured possessions, even our family? It takes a lot of faith, and this unnamed woman had it. Trustingly, she went to the prophet when her life seemed dark, perhaps hoping that, like Elijah, he could bring her son to life. Whether or not she expected this, she trusted God instead of turning her back on Him.

Do we have such faith? Can we turn to Him in our darkest hours? Remember, God often gives us surprising benefits when we trust fully in Him.

MORE THAN ENOUGH

*Then a man. . .brought the man of God
bread of the firstfruits, twenty loaves of barley bread, and
newly ripened grain in his knapsack. And he said, "Give it to the
people, that they may eat." But his servant said, "What? Shall
I set this before one hundred men?" He said again, "Give it
to the people, that they may eat; for thus says the LORD:
'They shall eat and have some left over.'"*

2 KINGS 4:42–43 NKJV

Famine had struck Gilgal. So when a man came to Elisha with his firstfruits offering, it was a momentous occasion. "Give the holy offering to the hungry people," Elisha commanded, handing his servant a terrible problem. *How can I choose who should get one of these small loaves?* Gehazi wondered. *And even so, would those who got one have enough? Not likely!* When he confronted him, the prophet commanded his servant to obey and pass the loaves around. There would be more than enough.

We don't know how, but the small loaves not only filled one hundred men—there were some left over, too. Does it sound like another miracle you know well?

God knows our needs and cares and sends us help in the right time. Does it seem too little too late? Let Him multiply, and it will be more than enough.

A CHANGED MAN

Now Naaman was commander of the army of the king of
Aram. He was a great man in the sight of his master and highly
regarded, because through him the LORD had given victory
to Aram. He was a valiant soldier, but he had leprosy. . . .
So he went down and dipped himself in the Jordan seven
times, as the man of God had told him, and his flesh was
restored and became clean like that of a young boy.

2 KINGS 5:1, 14

A powerful soldier, Naaman, was laid low by a skin disease,
though it probably was not the same one we call leprosy today.
In Israel, such an outward affliction was seen as being a sign
of sin. It's not surprising, therefore, that when Naaman's wife's
servant, a captured Israelite, heard of her master's trouble, she
suggested that he travel to her homeland to see the prophet
Elisha.

Full of hope, the commander went to his king, asking permission to leave his post for a time. Because he valued his
soldier, King Ben-Hadad of Aram (Syria) put all his authority
in train to help him. But instead of sending him to a prophet,
Ben-Hadad sent Naaman to a king: Jehoram of Israel. Perhaps this was wise, as there had been minor border conflicts
between his nation and Israel, though officially the two coun-
tries were at peace.

Naaman set out, carrying silver, gold, and plenty of clothes,
along with a letter introducing him to Israel's king. Jehoram

must have been something of a drama king, for when he read the letter, he immediately went into his theatrical act. First he tore his clothes (we can all only hope it wasn't his best duds). "Who am I to heal anyone of leprosy?" he demanded. Then he had an idea: "Aha! The king of Aram is looking to start a quarrel with me!" Nothing like assuming the worst in any situation: The king figured he was facing a potential war.

When the prophet Elisha heard the news, he took it calmly and sent to the king, suggesting that he send Naaman along to him. He'd show him what Israel's prophet could do. So the king sent Naaman back north, to the prophet's house in Samaria.

Naaman and his impressive retinue pulled up at the prophet's home. But they didn't get greeted the way they expected. Instead of being graciously received by the prophet, a messenger appeared before them and told the leper to go down to the Jordan River and wash in it seven times.

The important warrior felt rage course through his body. He'd expected something a lot more impressive than a mere message. And weren't the rivers of his native land better than the muddy Jordan? he asked. He stomped away in a huff.

Naaman couldn't see the futility of his attitude, but his servants could. Wouldn't it be worth anything to be rid of his disease? So what if he had to wash in the Jordan instead of another river? They convinced the man to do as the prophet said. So Naaman went to the Jordan, dipped himself in it seven times, and was healed. Could the prophet have required anything simpler?

After his healing, Naaman recognized the Lord as God

and dedicated himself to His service. He was truly a changed man. He even offered Elisha a gift. Perhaps mindful of the warrior's earlier attitude, the prophet would not even let him imagine he'd purchased his healing.

Maybe the commonplace attitude that sin caused leprosy was not so far off. Naaman certainly had some attitude problems. Wrapped up in himself, he almost missed out on being healed. In addition to having the skin problem, the warrior was self-important. The attitude showed itself in his hot-tempered rejection of the help he needed.

Do we almost miss God's greatest blessings because we're so caught up in ourselves that we can't even see them coming? Let's remember the example of Naaman, turn, and serve the Lord completely.

"Naaman's leprosy will cling to you and to your descendants forever." Then Gehazi went from Elisha's presence and he was leprous, as white as snow.

2 KINGS 5:27

After the healed commander Naaman left Elisha, the prophet's servant decided his master had been too easy on the Gentile. Elisha had flatly turned down the offer of a gift. But Gehazi decided he'd like to have something, so he followed the Aramean and told him that two prophets had come to visit, and Elisha needed a talent of silver and two festal garments.

The unsuspecting soldier gave him the money and the garments without question. Then he sent two of his own men back with Gehazi. When the three arrived at Elisha's house, the servant grabbed his booty and hurried Naaman's servants away.

Didn't Gehazi work for a prophet? How could he think he'd keep his wrongdoing from a man who could see through him? As soon as he saw his servant, the prophet asked where he'd been.

"Nowhere," the servant answered.

Elisha told him what he'd been doing and announced that Naaman's leprosy would cling to him and his descendants forever. Gehazi left, white as snow from the disease.

Greed may not make us leprous, at least not on the surface,

but it will damage our hearts and spirits as certainly as leprosy ruined Gehazi's skin. Are we careful to be honest?

FLOATING METAL

But as one was felling a beam, the axe head fell into the water: and he cried, and said, Alas, master! for it was borrowed. And the man of God said, Where fell it? And he shewed him the place. And he cut down a stick, and cast it in thither; and the iron did swim.
2 KINGS 6:5–6 KJV

Israel's prophets' school was involved in a building project, adding more space to their communal home. They went down to the Jordan to fell some trees to build the addition.

One of the men dropped his ax head into the water and cried out to Elisha, for an ax was a valuable and hard-to-find item, and the man had borrowed this one. These were not wealthy men, and its replacement would have been a problem. Not only that, the work could not go on as effectively without the tool.

So the prophet tossed a stick into the water to recover the iron ax head. Under normal circumstances, an ax head never would have floated, but by God's power, the metal did float, and the man was able to recover the valuable tool.

Is our need great? We can count on God for help, though the way seems impossible. We know where to turn when troubles would stop us in our tracks. Let's turn to the One who can even make metal float.

CAPTURED!

Behold, the mountain was full of horses and chariots of fire round about Elisha. And when they came down to him, Elisha prayed unto the LORD, and said, Smite this people, I pray thee, with blindness. And he smote them with blindness according to the word of Elisha.
2 KINGS 6:17–18 KJV

Israel was at war, and one of their best intelligence officers was the prophet Elisha. He would warn Israel's king not to send his army to certain places, because their enemies would be there. It was driving the king of Aram crazy! At first he thought there was a traitor in his ranks, until one of his officers explained that the prophet had been his downfall. So Aram's king ordered that Elisha should be captured. When intelligence reported the prophet was in Dothan, a strong force of men with chariots went to surround the city.

Elisha's new servant saw the men and their machines and warned the prophet. Despairingly, he asked what they should do.

"Fear not," Elisha answered. "For they that be with us are more than they that be with them" (6:16 KJV) Then he prayed for God to open his servant's eyes, and the man saw hills full of horses and chariots surrounding his master. God's army protected His prophet.

When the opposing army began to attack, Elisha had a battle plan: He prayed, asking God to blind his attackers. God responded. Then Elisha slipped into the ranks of the blind men and told them to follow him. He led them to his fortress hometown, Samaria, where they regained their sight.

When Israel's king heard of this, he asked if he should strike down the formerly blind soldiers. But Elisha declared that just as a king would not strike down those he'd already captured, Israel should allow these men to live. After providing a great feast for the captives, the king sent them home to Aram.

Because of the prophet's compassion, the raids that had plagued Israel for so long ended.

Elisha was a particularly effective peacemaker, and he never fought a battle, killed a man, or met with a king's representative. All his opponents suffered was temporary blindness.

When we face enemies, or even just troublesome people, are we constantly set on battle? Or are we open to a firm but gentler solution? Sometimes kindness has a powerful impact on others, when warfare would only antagonize and destroy. God provides the wisdom that will help us know when to use each. Are we listening to Him?

SECOND CHANCE

So it was, as they were burying a man, that suddenly they spied a band of raiders; and they put the man in the tomb of Elisha; and when the man was let down and touched the bones of Elisha, he revived and stood on his feet.

2 KINGS 13:21 NKJV

Following a fifty-year ministry, Elisha died and was buried.

Every spring, Moabite raiders dropped in on Israel to pick up a few things they weren't entitled to. The Israelites were not particularly successful at fighting back. In fact, they were better at running than defending themselves. So when raiders happened by a grave site, the men who were burying another man there simply dropped the body into Elisha's tomb for safekeeping.

How amazed the grave diggers must have been when their friend revived and stood up, perfectly healthy because his defunct body had touched the prophet's. How many other hopeful Israelites brought dead bodies to touch the prophet in the days that followed?

Scripture doesn't tell us why this man was revived or what happened to him. What did he make of his second opportunity at earthly life?

God may not bring us back from death, but He gives us second chances, too. What do we do with them?

MISPLACED TRUST?

And it came to pass on a certain night that the angel of the LORD
went out, and killed in the camp of the Assyrians one hundred
and eighty-five thousand; and when people arose early in the
morning, there were the corpses—all dead. So Sennacherib
king of Assyria departed and went away, returned home,
and remained at Nineveh. Now it came to pass, as he was
worshiping in the temple of Nisroch his god, that his
sons Adrammelech and Sharezer struck him down with
the sword; and they escaped into the land of Ararat.
Then Esarhaddon his son reigned in his place.

2 KINGS 19:35–37 NKJV

Assyria had attacked and conquered Israel and now was
looking in Judah's direction. Before the battle for Jerusalem
began, the Assyrian king Sennacherib sent his supreme commander, his chief officer, and his field commander to Israel
to intimidate the small nation. Hadn't they seen what he'd
done to the nations around them? the field commander, their
spokesman, asked. How could Israel hold out? Why not give
up now, make a bargain with Sennacherib, and join Assyria
in battle against other nations? The commander made certain
the people of Jerusalem heard these words, as he spoke to
Hezekiah's representatives. "Hezekiah and the Lord cannot
protect you," was the gist of his message.

When King Hezekiah received reports of that message,
he tore his clothes, sent for two of his best men and the top

priests, and had them dress in sackcloth, a sign of mourning and repentance. Then he sent these trusted men to Isaiah the prophet, to ask him to pray for the nation. According to Assyrian records, Sennacherib had already taken forty-six fortified Judean cities when his eye fell on the nation's capital, Jerusalem.

Isaiah replied to his king with comforting words: They should not fear. The Lord had heard the terrible blasphemies spoken by the Assyrian official, who had dared to compare other nations' idols with the Lord. God would take care of everything, the prophet assured Hezekiah. King Sennacherib would hear a certain bad report and return to his own country. There he would die by the sword.

Hezekiah received a second message from Assyria, denigrating God. The faithful king went to the temple and began to pray, glorifying God and asking for deliverance. Later, he got a message from Isaiah, confirming and expanding upon the original promise. Assyria would be destroyed. But Hezekiah received a promise that though two harvests would be affected by the Assyrian attack, by the third, Israel would be planting as usual. Jerusalem would be saved by God, who would defend it without a battle.

That very night, the angel of the Lord quietly went into the Assyrian camp and put to death 185,000 men. The next morning, when the dead bodies were discovered, Sennacherib quickly decided to remove his troops from Judah. He returned to his capital, Nineveh, and never bothered Judah again.

Isaiah's prophecy of the Assyrian king's death came true, too. Years later, when he was worshiping his pagan god, two of his sons came and cut him down with a sword. Another son succeeded him as king.

Hezekiah was an admirable man who stood firm for his Lord. Even a second attempt to scare him into compromise did not work—he turned again to God in worship instead of wasting his time in fear.

The God we trust in is as reliable today as He was in Hezekiah's time. He will fight our battles for us, and often, when we trust Him in remarkable circumstances, He will respond in an unexpected way. The problem we expected may never come to pass. The difficult issue will be resolved with no action on our part. Or the enemy will simply return home, never to bother us again.

Hezekiah's trust was not misplaced. Neither will ours be.

THE POWER OF PRAYER

*Hezekiah turned his face to the wall and prayed to the LORD,
"Remember, O LORD, how I have walked before you faithfully
and with wholehearted devotion and have done what
is good in your eyes." And Hezekiah wept bitterly.*

2 KINGS 20:2–3

Hezekiah was very ill when Isaiah visited him and told the king to put his house in order and prepare to die. Hearing this, the ruler did not give up but prayed to his Lord instead, reminding Him how devotedly he had served Him. Hezekiah cried bitterly.

Before Isaiah could walk out of the palace, God's word directed him to return to the king with a new message: God heard his prayer and would graciously heal him. Hezekiah would have fifteen years more of life on this earth. Only two things were required of the king: He had to go to the temple in three days, and he had to be treated with a fig poultice. The king had no trouble doing either.

Hezekiah must have been mighty in prayer and a truly faithful believer, for God did not contend with his estimate of his own faithfulness, and He did as the king asked.

Will our prayers be equally powerful because we have lived as faithful Christians? When we have believed with all our lives, we open ourselves to answered prayer.

Hezekiah had asked Isaiah, "What will be the sign that the LORD will heal me and that I will go up to the temple of the LORD on the third day from now?" Isaiah answered, "This is the LORD's sign to you that the LORD will do what he has promised: Shall the shadow go forward ten steps, or shall it go back ten steps?" "It is a simple matter for the shadow to go forward ten steps," said Hezekiah. "Rather, have it go back ten steps." Then the prophet Isaiah called upon the LORD, and the LORD made the shadow go back the ten steps it had gone down on the stairway of Ahaz.

2 KINGS 20:8–11

After God promised to heal King Hezekiah, the surprised ruler asked for a sign that the healing would occur. Because he was faithful, God complied. Isaiah promised that a shadow would move on the steps of Ahaz. But he left it up to the king as to which direction it would move. Hezekiah requested that the shadow do the harder move, going back ten steps, and God did as he requested.

God gave Hezekiah the sign he requested only because he was faithful. Have we so trusted Him that He can show us such grace, knowing we are not asking out of doubt?

HUMILITY AND TRUST

And, behold, there came a leper and worshipped him, saying,
Lord, if thou wilt, thou canst make me clean. And Jesus put forth
his hand, and touched him, saying, I will; be thou clean.
And immediately his leprosy was cleansed.
MATTHEW 8:2–3 KJV

After preaching the Sermon on the Mount, Jesus turned back toward Capernaum. As He headed toward the city, a leper came near, but perhaps not too near, since those who had leprosy were considered unclean and had to stay away from the "clean" people. Though this man was unable to go to temple and suffered physical and spiritual separation from his people, he came humbly, not angrily, to Jesus. Kneeling before Him in a worshipful attitude, he made his request with deference, leaving the ending up to the Savior.

The man's humility must have pleased the Master. He healed him in a moment, told him to offer the sacrifices required by the Law, and enjoined him not to tell anyone about what had happened. Can we doubt the former leper joyously obeyed?

When we face dire straits, can we react in similar humility and trust? Or are we so concerned about our need that we forget the power of our Lord and the respect He deserves?

IS SEEING BELIEVING?

*The centurion answered and said, Lord, I am not worthy
that thou shouldest come under my roof: but speak the word
only, and my servant shall be healed. For I am a man under
authority, having soldiers under me: and I say to this man, Go,
and he goeth; and to another, Come, and he cometh; and to my
servant, Do this, and he doeth it. When Jesus heard it,
he marvelled, and said to them that followed,
Verily I say unto you, I have not found
so great faith, no, not in Israel.*
MATTHEW 8:8–10 KJV

Romans would have considered themselves the master race in
Jesus' era. They had conquered most of the known world that
surrounded the Mediterranean Sea and some areas beyond it.
Many probably wouldn't have cared much about a servant's
illness, much less a Jewish teacher, even one who could heal.
What problem couldn't the power of Rome solve?

But this man, a leader of a hundred soldiers, was a real
leader. He cared enough for his paralyzed servant to humble
himself and go before Jesus. As a Gentile, his claim on the
Lord was tenuous, to say the least. So some of Jesus' fellow
Jews went to tell the Master that this God-fearing soldier
had helped them build a synagogue (see Luke 7:2–5).

But this man did not need such a testimony. His own
attitude was self-explanatory. He wouldn't even call Jesus
into his home, because he felt guilty, knowing it would make

the Master ceremonially unclean. Looking to his military background, he gave Jesus an idea: Heal the servant from a distance. If the Lord said it was done, the soldier could trust it would happen.

Jesus marveled at the man's faith, for even in Israel He'd not seen such trust. He healed the servant immediately.

Are we like the Israelites, who needed to see everything right before them, or can we trust like the faithful centurion? Though he came from another land, his trust was obviously in the Lord. What God said, he believed.

If we really believe, seeing is not all there is to believing.

And when Jesus was come into Peter's house,
he saw his wife's mother laid, and sick of a fever.
And he touched her hand, and the fever left her:
and she arose, and ministered unto them.

MATTHEW 8:14–15 KJV

Jesus healed not only the masses of people who came to Him with serious illnesses, but when He came to Peter's house and discovered Peter's mother-in-law suffering from a fever, He went to her, took her hand, and gently helped her up. The fever left her body.

Perhaps, knowing Jesus would be coming, she had lain in bed worrying about the preparations she could not make. For as soon as she felt healthy again, she rose to minister to Jesus and His men.

Is there an illness, either spiritual or physical, that is too small to gain Jesus' attention? Isn't He aware of all that goes on in this universe? Is there anything we can hide from Him? Let's bring all our cares before our Lord's throne and share any need that comes our way. Just as He lifted up Peter's mother-in-law, He can lift us up, too, if only we ask.

HE IS LORD!

Then he got into the boat and his disciples followed him.
Without warning, a furious storm came up on the lake,
so that the waves swept over the boat. But Jesus was sleeping.
The disciples went and woke him, saying, "Lord, save us! We're
going to drown!" He replied, "You of little faith, why are you so
afraid?" Then he got up and rebuked the winds and the waves,
and it was completely calm. The men were amazed
and asked, "What kind of man is this? Even the
winds and the waves obey him!"
MATTHEW 8:23–27

Since childhood, this has been a favorite drama of many Christians: the disciples battling the waves while Jesus sleeps and the wonderful miracle that follows. In a few short verses, we get a vivid picture. The master storytellers of scripture give us a brief, vibrant vignette of Jesus and His authority over nature.

Some of the men in the boat, probably the ones sailing it, were extremely familiar with the Sea of Galilee. Fishermen Peter and Andrew, John and James had doubtless sailed on this body of water since childhood. They understood the vagaries of its winds. For this sea lies between two ranges of hills and is about 700 feet below sea level, so the winds filling the sails of the first-century small fishing boats that plied this sea were erratic. Cool Mediterranean winds met the warm air in the sea's basin, and strong winds and sudden storms often resulted.

This was hardly the first sudden storm the fishermen had run into. They'd honed their sailing skills here. They'd sailed with a boat piled with a full catch and with one empty except for a few men. They made their livings from the sea's bountiful schools of fish.

Now these sailors probably called out sharply to one another as they sought to keep their boat under control: "Grab this line." "Do that." "Head into that wave, or we'll be swamped." The rest of the disciples probably huddled down, trying to stay out of their way and waiting to see what would happen. In a small, open vessel, at the best of times it would have been a very wet ride.

Perhaps some of the "landlubbers" first cried out to Jesus as the small vessel tipped first to one side then to the other and rose and fell on the churning waves. Water entered the boat. Fear filled their hearts, and their trust in the sailors waned. The fishermen were probably too busy looking to their boat to give thought to anything else. Or maybe Peter had shouted a command to the others to wake Jesus before they all drowned.

The fearful disciples had seen Jesus do miraculous healings, and in this dire situation, they turned to their exhausted Master, who slept on a pillow in the stern (see Mark 4:38). "Lord, save us! We're going to drown!" they cried.

Jesus awoke and took command, but first He reminded His disciples of their lack of faith. With Him there, what had they to fear? Realistically, would God really have ended this earthly mission by letting His Son's chosen men drown? Then He rebuked the wind and waves, and all was quiet.

The disciples had gotten what they asked for, yet they sat in the steady boat, stunned. Terrified, they asked each other who this was who could do such a miracle?

We may never set foot in a boat, but our lives are also filled with storms: emotional, physical, and spiritual. Like the disciples, we turn to Jesus for our answers. But are we surprised when He answers us in powerful ways? He is God. It was the only conclusion the disciples could come to as they watched the sun sparkle on a sea that lapped gently at the sides of the boat. It's the only conclusion we can come to based on the scriptural evidence and our own experiences with Him.

*When Jesus arrived at the official's home,
he saw the noisy crowd and heard the funeral music. "Get
out!" he told them. "The girl isn't dead; she's only asleep." But
the crowd laughed at him. After the crowd was put outside,
however, Jesus went in and took the girl by the hand,
and she stood up! The report of this miracle swept
through the entire countryside.*
MATTHEW 9:23–26 NLT

As soon as Jesus stepped off the boat that sailed the water
He'd just stilled, a crowd began to surround Him. Through
it pushed a man on a mission. Mark 5:22 tells us his name
was Jairus, and he was the synagogue leader—a man who
either performed administrative duties for his congregation
or held this as an honorary title. Whichever it was, he was an
important man. He came to Jesus trusting that He could heal
his only daughter. Jesus headed toward Jairus's home. But
before he could take many steps, a hurting woman stopped
Him with her need.

Hurry, hurry, hurry, Jairus must have been thinking.
While Jesus spoke a few words to the woman, men of his
own household came to tell Jairus his daughter was dead.
How the fond father's face and heart must have fallen. But
Jesus told him not to fear, just believe. Taking with them only
His closest disciples, Peter, James, and John, Jesus and Jairus
headed for the synagogue leader's home.

By the time Jesus reached that house, the flute players for the funeral had already been hired. The Lord told them and the wailing and crying crowd surrounding them to go home, for the child was simply asleep. They laughed at Him.

Inside, with the parents and His few disciples in attendance, Jesus took the child by one hand and said, "Little girl, I say to you, get up!" (Mark 5:41). She stood up and walked around, astonishing her parents and the disciples. After warning them not to tell anyone about this, Jesus told them to feed the girl and left.

But of course the story flew around the countryside. Who could resist passing on such a tale, and even if the parents kept silence, no one could miss the little girl who was once dead prancing around her family home, no doubt joyous at having received her life back.

Jairus came to Jesus with faith. But when he heard of his daughter's death, how grieved and hopeless he must have felt. Yet Jesus, honoring that first bit of faith, told him not to worry. "Hold on to your faith," was His message in this father's darkest hour.

That's the message Jesus gives to us, too. Nothing is impossible for Him, no situation too bleak for us to trust that His help will not change our lives. Let's hold on, no matter what lies before us.

ADMIT IT

*Just then a woman who had suffered for twelve years with
constant bleeding came up behind him. She touched the fringe
of his robe, for she thought, "If I can just touch his robe, I will
be healed." Jesus turned around, and when he saw her he said,
"Daughter, be encouraged! Your faith has made you well."
And the woman was healed at that moment.*
MATTHEW 9:20–22 NLT

As Jairus called Jesus away to heal his daughter, a poor woman
got up some courage. *If I can just touch his clothing, I will be
healed*, she thought. She wasn't looking for attention, just an
end to the bleeding that had made her ritually impure and
destroyed her life. Though she had sought out many doctors,
spending all her money, no healing resulted.

As her fingers reached out and touched the fabric, she felt
the bleeding stop. But instead of being a quiet testimony to
Jesus' power, her miracle was about to go public. For the Lord
turned around and asked who had touched Him. His disciples
made light of it, since a crowd pressed around Him, but
Jesus knew power had gone from Him. When the trembling
woman admitted what had happened, He confirmed her
healing with His words.

Sometimes we'd prefer a quiet testimony, perhaps only to
our friends. But Jesus wants the Good News spread. Are we
willing, like this woman, to admit to our healing?

SHRIVELED HEARTS

Then He said to the man,
"Stretch out your hand." And he stretched it out,
and it was restored as whole as the other.
MATTHEW 12:13 NKJV

As we read this single verse, we're likely to write it off as merely another minor miracle. But reading the context of this verse, we may come to another conclusion.

This was a confrontation between Jesus and the Pharisees, a small group of men who seemed to have godly devotion but had gotten caught up in traditions and formal observances rather than heartfelt faith. The Pharisees, who only numbered about six thousand in Jesus' day, had influence in the religious community. Some were even part of the Sanhedrin, the Jewish ruling body.

Doctrinally, Jesus usually agreed with the Pharisees, but here He takes them on. They wanted Him to wait until the end of the sabbath to heal, but He pointed out their inconsistency of thought: They allowed an animal to be rescued on the Sabbath but committed a man to suffering. Then, right in their faces, He healed the man with a shriveled hand.

The Pharisees didn't have a theology problem: They had a heart problem. Can we take them as an example of what not to do and instead love others as Jesus calls us to? Then neither our hearts nor spirits will be shriveled.

OUT OF LITTLE, MUCH

"Bring them here to me," he said.
And he directed the people to sit down on the grass.
Taking the five loaves and the two fish and looking up to
heaven, he gave thanks and broke the loaves. Then he gave them
to the disciples, and the disciples gave them to the people. They
all ate and were satisfied, and the disciples picked up twelve
basketfuls of broken pieces that were left over. The number
of those who ate was about five thousand men,
besides women and children.
MATTHEW 14:18–21

After hearing that His cousin, John the Baptist, had been beheaded, Jesus withdrew by boat to Bethsaida. But the crowds hounded Him, following on foot. Putting aside His own desires, the Master began healing the sick. Then, feeling compassion for all the people, He taught them until evening.

As the shadows lengthened, Jesus' disciples came to Him, suggesting that He send the people out to pick up some fast food before night came. In this out-of-the-way place, they reminded Him, there were few spots where His listeners could find any food at all, much less enough for such a crowd. Knowing full well what He planned to do, Jesus told them the people did not need to leave and asked the disciples to feed them.

Surprise must have filled their faces at that request, but

Andrew offered the best he had: He'd met a boy who had brought along five small barley loaves and a couple of fish. *But how could so little feed so many?* this faithful follower wondered. Despite the many healings they'd witnessed, the disciples seemingly had no clue what was about to occur.

Jesus commanded all the people to sit down, and the disciples passed on the message to the crowd. Five thousand men, not counting the women and children, plunked down in the dirt.

Jesus took the boy's pitifully small amount of food. After giving thanks, He broke the loaves and passed them to the disciples, who handed them out. How amazed everyone must have been when five loaves turned into well over five thousand, and two fish fed all the thousands sitting in the grass around Jesus. Everyone had a full meal out of one boy's small dinner.

Jesus told His disciples to gather the uneaten pieces. The Jews of that era saw bread as a gift from God that should not be wasted—its scraps were always gathered at the end of a meal. The twelve each filled a small basket with bread and fish leftovers.

The meal had not started with the most impressive of ingredients. This would have been a poor boy's dinner, not the finer bread that the wealthy consumed. But even if the food was not gourmet quality, the miracle the spectators saw performed was more than worth their time. As they ate, astonished friends must have chattered about the day's healings and about the multiplication of the bare essentials of a meal into catering for the whole crowd. It had been an eventful day, and what a joyous one for those who had been healed.

Out of such a meager meal, Jesus fed many, to the surprise of His disciples. Do we too expect so little from our Lord that we doubt His ability to solve our crises? Though we bring our needs before Him, do we feel we also need to describe the solution to Him? Like the disciples, we need to ask ourselves whom we address here: Is He Lord, or simply a person? Does He rule the universe, or everything but the universe of our hearts?

He brings much out of little. He can do that with our hearts, too, if we are willing.

WALK ON WATER

*Immediately he made the disciples get into the boat
and go before him to the other side, while he dismissed the
crowds. And after he had dismissed the crowds, he went up on
the mountain by himself to pray. When evening came, he was
there alone, but the boat by this time was a long way from the
land, beaten by the waves, for the wind was against them. And
in the fourth watch of the night he came to them, walking on
the sea. But when the disciples saw him walking on the sea,
they were terrified, and said, "It is a ghost!" and they
cried out in fear. But immediately Jesus spoke to them,
saying, "Take heart; it is I. Do not be afraid."*
MATTHEW 14:22–27 ESV

Right after feeding more than five thousand, Jesus dispatched
the disciples in their boat and sent the crowds home. Then He
continued what was probably His original purpose in going
off alone: He went to pray.

As dusk settled over the sky, Jesus stood alone on the
shore. His disciples were having a rough time sailing. The
wind was coming pretty much from the direction in which
they were headed, so they had to tack back and forth, moving
a little at a time toward their goal. In addition, the waves
worked against them. Between three and six in the morning,
the tired and wet disciples saw Jesus coming toward them,
walking on the water.

Water isn't exactly the sidewalk anyone would expect a

person to walk on. Terrified at the sight of Jesus on the water, the disciples came to a quick and somewhat logical solution: They were looking at a ghost. After all, a ghost would be lightweight enough to appear above the water. They cried out in fear.

Jesus soothed them, assuring them He was no ghost and telling them not to fear.

Practical Peter wanted proof. "Lord, if it is you, command me to come to you on the water," he demanded (14:28 ESV).

Jesus called him to Himself, and courageous Peter stepped out of the boat onto the water. Watching Jesus, the disciple walked toward Him. His trust lay fully in the Lord, and as much as it was a miracle that Jesus walked on water, it was even more so that Peter could do so through His power. But as he got out into the whipping wind, Peter began to fear and started to sink into the water. "Lord, save me," he cried out (14:30 ESV).

Jesus immediately grabbed hold of the sinking disciple. Chastising Peter for his doubts, He saved him from a watery death. As soon as the two men got in the boat, the wind stopped roaring in their ears and the water was calm.

All twelve disciples, understanding what this meant, worshiped Him. For there remained no doubt in their minds that one who could do these things was God.

When we read this story, whom do we see ourselves as? Is it the eleven disciples huddling in the boat, afraid of the man who walks on the sea? Could He be Jesus or an evil being? Or do we see ourselves as foolhardy Peter, who gathers up his courage, steps out of the boat, but is distracted by the sights around him and begins to sink?

The truth of the matter is that whichever disciple we are, we're prone to failure. Under our own power, we can never effectively live the Christian life. But when Jesus fills our hearts and spirits with His Spirit and we look steadily at Him, we too can walk on water. We may never set foot on a sea, but spiritually we can do things we'd never done before.

Ready to look Jesus straight in the eye and step out of the boat?

DOING LAPS

*Then Jesus called his disciples to him and said, "I have
compassion on the crowd because they have been with me now
three days and have nothing to eat. And I am unwilling to send
them away hungry, lest they faint on the way." And the disciples
said to him, "Where are we to get enough bread in such a desolate
place to feed so great a crowd?" And Jesus said to them, "How
many loaves do you have?" They said, "Seven, and a few small
fish." And directing the crowd to sit down on the ground, he took
the seven loaves and the fish, and having given thanks he broke
them and gave them to the disciples, and the disciples gave them
to the crowds. And they all ate and were satisfied. And they took
up seven baskets full of the broken pieces left over.*
MATTHEW 15:32–37 ESV

Sometimes we may feel as if God has us doing laps: Just when
we think we have a faith concept down pat, it returns to our
lives. Perhaps that's the way at least one of the disciples felt
when compassionate Jesus asked how they should feed the
four thousand folks who'd come to Him for healing. He'd
healed many bodies, and now, after three days, even those
who had brought food along were out of it. So Jesus planned
to feed the whole crowd before Him.

Haven't we already done this for a larger group? the more
alert of the Twelve must have been thinking. Someone asked
where they could get a truckload of bread anyway. Yet when
Jesus requested them, the disciples immediately directed Jesus

to a smaller quantity of loaves and fish. Again Jesus gave thanks and started to distribute the food. A second time, everyone ate and was satisfied. The disciples picked up the leftovers.

This time, the surprise must not have been so great. Jesus had done it before, and doubtless word of the previous miracle had spread. But surely the recipients were thankful they'd go home with full stomachs.

The disciples probably never forgot Jesus' compassionate lesson. A second time they'd seen Him care for those who needed food. Though the crowd was sometimes irritating and certainly interfered with His plans, Jesus did not hold it against them. Instead, He gave them all they required.

Have we done laps lately? Is God trying to impress something on our hearts? Let's not become resentful. Instead, let's benefit from it by taking the message to heart and making it a permanent part of our spiritual lives.

"Nevertheless, lest we offend them, go to the sea, cast in a hook, and take the fish that comes up first. And when you have opened its mouth, you will find a piece of money; take that and give it to them for Me and you."

MATTHEW 17:27 NKJV

When we read this story of Peter's faux pas, we feel for him. After all, he meant well enough, trying to make it clear to the Pharisees that Jesus was a faithful Jew. Perhaps it never entered Peter's mind that Jesus wouldn't pay the temple tax established by Moses and repeated throughout Israel's history.

Jesus points out to His disciple that as the Son of David and the Son of God, it is not for Him to have to pay a tax. How foolish Peter must have felt when the Lord reminded him He was the honored one, not just another worshiper. Yet Jesus will not unnecessarily offend the Pharisees, so He provides the money both for Himself and Peter in a miraculous way—that had to be the most unusual catch Peter ever had, and he'd certainly never forget it.

Do we recognize Jesus as the powerful Lord He is, or when we witness, do we bend the truth a bit so people will think kindly of Him? If so, in the end, we may do more damage to His reputation than we expected.

In the morning, as [Jesus] was returning to the city, he became
hungry. And seeing a fig tree by the wayside, he went to it
and found nothing on it but only leaves. And he said
to it, "May no fruit ever come from you again!"
And the fig tree withered at once.
MATTHEW 21:18–19 ESV

On the day following His triumphal entry into Jerusalem,
Jesus headed from Bethany, where He'd spent the night, to
Jerusalem. Hungry, when He saw a fig tree heavy with leaves,
which seemed to indicated that, though it was early for fruit,
this tree should be bearing. But when He neared the tree, it
was barren.

In an unusual event, Jesus cursed the tree. None would eat
from it again. When He and His disciples passed that way
the next day, the tree was withered (see Mark 11:20).

Some scholars assume the fig tree is a symbol of Israel
and that this is a curse upon that nation, but in the text that
directly follows, Jesus speaks instead of faith rather than
doubt and of the power of believing prayer.

The first application may not closely touch our lives. The
second will. Do we have faith that God's works will come to
pass, or do we doubt? How will that affect our prayers?

*Now from the sixth hour there was darkness over all the
land until the ninth hour. And about the ninth hour Jesus cried
out with a loud voice, saying, "Eli, Eli, lema sabachthani?"
that is, "My God, my God, why have you forsaken me?"*
MATTHEW 27:45–46 ESV

Following a kangaroo court trial, Jesus had been forced to
march from Pilate's residence in Jerusalem to Golgotha.
Mocking voices followed Him to the cross. Scripture provides all the details of the people around Him, and every
event is laid out. As if on a stage, the entire history of the
morning plays out before our eyes. But around noon, a
mysterious event occurs when a strange darkness covers the
land.

The brief description of the event in scripture gives us few
clues about how the miraculous darkness happened. "The sun
stopped shining," Luke simply reports (23:45). Many assume
this was an eclipse of the sun, but if so, surely the timing of
it was still perfectly miraculous, for it began at the perfect
moment and lasted only three hours, the time during which
Jesus was on the cross. God's Son was mercifully hidden from
the light of day as He suffered for humanity's sin.

The darkness that covered the earth as Jesus suffered
certainly symbolizes sin and the removal of light from the
Jews who did not accept this permanent sacrifice for their sin.
But did the people who observed it pass it off as a "business as

usual" eclipse, or did they recognize the connection between the crucifixion and the sky's darkening? Scripture does not tell us that as He died any Jews turned with fear or recognition of their own unbelief. But some time after all the events were ended, a large number of priests came to the faith (see Acts 6:7). Perhaps they remembered Amos 8:9–10 NIV: " 'In that day,' declares the Sovereign LORD, 'I will make the sun go down at noon and darken the earth in broad daylight. . . . I will make that time like mourning for an only son and the end of it like a bitter day.' "

Perhaps the mercy of darkness that covered the Lord's suffering is also shown to us today. For who among us can really stand a clear view of what our sin cost God's Son? When we think of it, even at Easter, don't our eyes turn down in shame, our spirits seek to escape the enormity of our own failings? Some sin we can admit, but the whole of it would topple our spirits in a moment. Can we bear the full knowledge that is was for our every wrong that He cried out in pain, "My God, my God, why have you forsaken me?"

Our merciful God confronts us with just enough knowledge of our sin to bring us to Himself. The pain we feel when we recognize our own wrongs or the emptiness that draws us to Him may wrench our lives, but it does not destroy us. In His grace, He will not give us more than we can bear.

But we do need to recognize that our sins were paid for on the cross. For us Jesus suffered and died. And we must acknowledge the grace that paid for it all and demands every bit of our lives in return. As we understand that, the darkness is no longer dark, for we live in the brightness of eternity with Jesus, our Lord and Savior.

THE HOLIEST PLACE

And when Jesus had cried out again in a loud voice,
he gave up his spirit. At that moment the curtain of the
temple was torn in two from top to bottom.
MATTHEW 27:50–51

At the moment Jesus died, the world changed forever. Believers no longer needed to make animal sacrifices for their sins. The final sacrifice had been made, and through Jesus, people now had direct access to God.

In the Jewish temple, a curtain separated the holy of holies, the holiest part of the temple, from the rest of the worship center. Only the high priest could go there, and then only once yearly, with a blood sacrifice. The holy of holies was an awesome place containing, among other things, the ark of the covenant, which held the tablets of the Law and Aaron's rod, which had budded in the wilderness when the Israelites questioned Moses' authority. When the Jews thought of the holy of holies, they understood how far they were from God's perfection. And they feared God because they understood that He could not tolerate their sin.

God opened this holiest place to all His people through the sacrifice of Jesus. That wasn't because God had changed.

He was still as holy as ever, as awesome as He'd been before. But now humanity's sins had been permanently forgiven through His Son, and people could approach Him with confidence. They no longer needed to walk into the holy of holies with fear. The blood of the Son had been shed to bring before God's throne those who believe in Him.

The temple curtain that tore from top to bottom was no flimsy bit of chiffon, but a thick, durable linen, in which the threads had been doubled over numerous times. No stray wind flew through the temple and caused this. No priest accidentally caused any run in the fabric. God was intentionally and personally ending the separation between His people and Himself. After all, who else could rip forty cubits of fabric from the top?

Did the priests wonder how and why this happened? Is that one reason why, in the book of Acts, so many of them came to faith in Jesus as the Messiah? Perhaps, like the centurion, they saw proof that this was surely God's Son.

Through Jesus' sacrifice, we have direct access to God, the Holy One. But do we sufficiently recognize His holiness, or are we quick to treat Him as a heavenly Santa who should bow to our wishes? If so, we are not worshiping the Lord of the Bible. Though He gives us direct access to His throne room, He is not pleased if we treat Him lightly.

The Lord we serve is as awesome as His holiest of places showed Him to be. Do we treat Him with great respect? Let's not forget who He really is, for though He loves us deeply, He is still the Lord of all.

The earth shook and the rocks split.
The tombs broke open and the bodies of many holy people
who had died were raised to life. They came out of the tombs,
and after Jesus' resurrection they went into the
holy city and appeared to many people.
MATTHEW 27:51–53

Just as the temple curtain tore from top to bottom, the earth convulsed, breaking open tombs. This was not simply a geological coincidence. Rocks split, and the heavy stones that barred the way into first-century Jewish tombs may have rolled away. This heaving of the ground occurred just at the end of Jesus' earthly life, along with another, more stunning event. According to the book of Matthew, the only Gospel to record this, after Jesus' resurrection many believers were also resurrected. Were they given life for a few minutes, a few hours, a few days, or much longer? We don't know. But imagine the shock it must have been for loving relatives to suddenly see Uncle Samuel or Aunt Rebekah alive again! What were they to make of it?

In case the questioning relatives had doubts of their own sanity, many others saw the resurrected ones, too. But the event meant more than a return to friends and family. With Jesus' resurrection, death ended not only for Himself, but for all who trust in Him. The risen believers picture the work His resurrection accomplishes.

No one in Jerusalem that week could have ignored the events that took place when Jesus died. Those who came up with an explanation for the temple curtain ripping so unexpectedly might also have discounted the earthquake but would have been hard pressed to explain this resurrection reported by multiple witnesses. Only a determined but illogical decision to suppress the truth would have covered it over. And that's what many people in Jerusalem must have chosen.

God probably has not brought a loved one to life to get our attention, but He has placed many indicators in our paths that show us the truth about Jesus and His resurrection. Will we deny them? Then our hearts are as stubbornly against Him as were some of those first-century Jews'.

EMPTY TOMB!

Toward the dawn of the first day of the week,
Mary Magdalene and the other Mary went to see the tomb.
And behold, there was a great earthquake, for an angel of the
Lord descended from heaven and came and rolled back the
stone and sat on it. His appearance was like lightning, and his
clothing white as snow. And for fear of him the guards trembled
and became like dead men. But the angel said to the women, "Do
not be afraid, for I know that you seek Jesus who was crucified.
He is not here, for he has risen, as he said. Come, see the place
where he lay. Then go quickly and tell his disciples that he has
risen from the dead, and behold, he is going before
you to Galilee; there you will see him."
MATTHEW 28:1–7 ESV

Another earthquake heralded what may have been the greatest surprise for both the nearest disciples and the occasional followers of Jesus. Though He'd warned about His death and spoken of His resurrection, clearly they had not quite understood what to expect. The women who went to His tomb the day after the sabbath, though faithful followers, were probably fairly clueless about what the future held. But it was to the women that news of the greatest event in church history was given.

The two Marys came to the tomb with some other women, according to the other Gospels (see Mark 16:1; Luke 24:10). As they neared the grave, the earth moved as an angel of the Lord came down (Luke and John report there were two angels). At least the angel solved one problem the women had discussed: How would they open the tomb? For the angel sat on the stone that should have barred their way but had been moved aside by his power. How they'd have access to the body was the least important issue now, for they received perplexing news from the terrifying messenger: Jesus was no longer there.

The guards who had been placed on tomb duty to make sure no believers took Jesus' body trembled at the sight of an angelic presence and "became like dead men." Once the guards were peacefully out of the way, the angel gave his message. And he sent the women to the Eleven, to tell them about the Resurrection and send them to Galilee.

Fear and joy filled the women's hearts as they headed off to tell the disciples. On their way to see Peter, John, and the others, Jesus met them, told them not to fear, and repeated the angel's message for the Eleven.

Not surprisingly, when Jesus' closest disciples heard the story, they had their doubts. They hadn't expected this, despite what Jesus had told them before His death. But Peter and John went to check out the story anyway. Thunderstruck by the physical proof there, they believed.

Faithful Mary Magdalene stayed behind, weeping at the loss of her Lord. Because she remained, she had the first opportunity to see the risen Christ, though it took her awhile to recognize Him.

Those who witnessed the truth of the Resurrection could hardly believe their eyes. The events that followed proved that in reality seeing is not always believing. But we can be sympathetic to their plight. The news they received was unlike anything that had happened before. Even the return to life they'd seen with Lazarus could not have prepared them for a crucified man being resurrected. They'd seen Jesus' corpse, and unlike some modern skeptics, they knew that He could not spring to life simply because He'd been left in a cool place.

To us today, the news of the Resurrection can seem beyond belief. But it is the one great proof that Jesus was who He said He was and that He does what He claimed He could. The evidence is aimed at faith, not scientific proof, but God has given us all we need to know. Will we believe, or will we stand with the skeptical first-century Jews who never looked inside the empty tomb?

SHOUTING SPIRIT

And immediately there was in their synagogue a man
with an unclean spirit. And he cried out, "What have you to do
with us, Jesus of Nazareth? Have you come to destroy us?
I know who you are—the Holy One of God." But Jesus
rebuked him, saying, "Be silent, and come out of him!"
And the unclean spirit, convulsing him and crying out
with a loud voice, came out of him.
MARK 1:23–26 ESV

No sooner had Jesus begun His teaching ministry in Capernaum than the voice of a man with an evil spirit interrupted Him. Though his words seem to praise Jesus, they are merely an identification of His power and authority—something to be feared by evil spirits, as this one rightly assesses. In agony, the spirit cries out against the Holy One.

Jesus immediately quelled the interruption. The words politely translated "be silent" literally mean "be muzzled." Then he freed the man from the demonic being. In a noisy manner, the demon left the man's body.

Jesus' audience had been marveling at His authority in teaching; now they were amazed. A man with little formal education, who could teach this way and free people from demons! Their gossip filled Galilee in short order.

Do we recognize Jesus' authority over the spirit, as they did? Or do our spirits shout against Him? If so, we need to come to Him for cleansing so we can walk in His ways.

"But that you may know that the Son of Man has authority on earth to forgive sins. . . ." He said to the paralytic, "I tell you, get up, take your mat and go home." He got up, took his mat and walked out in full view of them all. This amazed everyone and they praised God, saying, "We have never seen anything like this!"
MARK 2:10–12

Though the paralyzed man lay on a mat, unable to help himself, he had four good friends or family members who went to great lengths to help him. For when they discovered that the way to Jesus was blocked by a crowd, they climbed on the roof and dug through it so they could lower the man down to Jesus for healing.

What a shock it must have been for the people in the room with Jesus to hear the noise of the roof removal, then see the man lowered down on his mat. Perhaps willing arms reached up to grab the one who could do nothing but hope nobody dropped him.

The faith of his friends encouraged Jesus to heal the man. "Son, your sins are forgiven," He declared (2:5).

While the hurting man looked on in horror, the teachers of the law started a debate with Jesus on whether He could forgive sins. Here this helpless fellow lay, and the religious men wanted to start an argument! The man on the mat probably wanted to break in, "Pardon me, but could you let

Him heal me first!"

Not losing sight of the importance of this healing, Jesus quickly asked which was easier, to tell someone his sins were forgiven, or to heal him? But to prove His point, He declared the man healed, then told him to take up his mat and go home.

While the crowd was praising God, how much more loudly the four friends must have extolled Him. The one whom they'd lowered on a mat could walk freely and strongly and live in a no longer sin-damaged body.

Who are we? The paralyzed man, who had lost his life to sin? The loving friends, who worked hard to see him healed? Or the litigious teachers, nailing down the theology of the issue before the man can be helped?

What will most glorify God today? Our personally turning from sin? Helping others come to faith and turn from wrongdoing? Or discussing the theological implications? Having good theology is important. But it does not substitute for the other two. Loving action that recognizes the claims of Jesus is more critical than senseless debates. When we know His power, we live in it.

A LEGION OF DEMONS

And Jesus asked him, "What is your name?"
He replied, "My name is Legion, for we are many." And
he begged him earnestly not to send them out of the country.
Now a great herd of pigs was feeding there on the hillside, and
they begged him, saying, "Send us to the pigs; let us enter them."
So he gave them permission. And the unclean spirits came out,
and entered the pigs, and the herd, numbering about two
thousand, rushed down the steep bank into the
sea and were drowned in the sea.

MARK 5:9–13 ESV

Had the media existed then, this story could have made headlines around the world. Even without them, you can bet descriptions flew around the Gerasene region for weeks. Gossip and storytelling took the place of media in that age.

Jesus and His disciples had crossed to this gentile area, and no sooner had Jesus debarked than a man with an evil spirit emerged from the cavern tomb where he lived. His friends and neighbors had tried to chain him, perhaps for their protection and his own, but he had broken the bonds. No one could control him, and according to the book of Luke, he did not even wear clothes (see 8:27). As he lived among the tombs, he cut himself and cried out day and night.

This miserable man ran to Jesus and fell on his knees. The demon within him shouted at the top of his voice, "What have you to do with me, Jesus, Son of the Most High God? I adjure you by God, do not torment me" (Mark 5:7 ESV). How ironic that a demon would claim the name of God, whom he had refused to serve. But though humans could deny Jesus was Messiah, no demon could ignore His real identity.

The demon spoke these words because Jesus had already been commanding him to leave the man, and he didn't like it. Calmly, Jesus asked his name. "Legion," he replied, for the man had many demons controlling him. This was the beginning of a spiritual battle, for in the first century, knowing a name was believed to mean one had power over the named one.

Recognizing the inevitable, the demons asked Jesus not to send them back to hell, but to allow them to stay in the pagan country they now inhabited and to let them enter a herd of pigs feeding on a nearby hillside.

Jesus allowed them to enter the pigs, and they immediately took them over as they had overtaken the man. The troublesome demons caused the two thousand unclean beasts to rush down the steep bank and drown in the sea.

The herdsmen ran to tell the news to all they met, and soon Jesus had a crowd around Him. When they saw the once demon-possessed man sitting there clothed and in his right mind, they became so fearful they begged Jesus to leave.

The man who had been healed wanted to go back into Israel with Jesus, but He left him in his hometown as a testimony to God. The excited man must have immediately started to tell his neighbors, who had already heard all the gossip. His experience would have been hard to hide, anyway.

There are always at least two ways of thinking about

spiritual things. The demon-possessed man's neighbors could have looked at his healing and thought, *How wonderful! A man who can do that is certainly worth following.* But they didn't. Perhaps because of the loss of the pigs—was their owner a big man in town?—they worried about what might happen. They couldn't wait to get this "troublemaker" away. How many other healings did they miss because they were unwilling hosts?

Jesus has power over all spirits. But the heart that resists Him may well miss out on the good He wants to perform in that life. God will woo the sinner, but He will not bash down doors. He calls us with His grace, but some still remain on their sinful path.

God is calling you, wooing you with His grace. Will you fall on your knees and worship Him, like the healed man who had nothing to lose, or will you cling to your pigs and lose the best God offers?

*Then they brought to Him one who was deaf
and had an impediment in his speech, and they begged
Him to put His hand on him. And He took him aside from
the multitude, and put His fingers in his ears, and He spat
and touched his tongue. Then, looking up to heaven, He sighed,
and said to him, "Ephphatha," that is, "Be opened."
Immediately his ears were opened, and the impediment of
his tongue was loosed, and he spoke plainly.*
MARK 7:32–35 NKJV

The man brought before Jesus this day had double trouble: deafness and a speech impediment. How limited his life was. He was trapped inside himself, with few ways of communicating with the world.

Then someone brought him to Jesus and begged the Master to heal him. Jesus took the man aside, perhaps so that he'd not be overwhelmed by the noise of the crowds about him.

Jesus put his fingers in the man's ears, spit and touched the man's tongue, and looked up into heaven. He commanded the ears to open, and the man's ears began to function and his voice spoke out plainly. In a few moments he'd been perfectly healed and Jesus had fulfilled Isaiah's prophecy that the ears of the deaf would be unstopped and the tongue of the dumb would sing (see Isaiah 35:5–6).

We who have our voices and the ability to hear, are our faculties open to God? Are we praising Him with all He's given us?

And some people brought to him a blind man and begged him to touch him. And he took the blind man by the hand and led him out of the village, and when he had spit on his eyes and laid his hands on him, he asked him, "Do you see anything?" And he looked up and said, "I see men, but they look like trees, walking." Then Jesus laid his hands on his eyes again; and he opened his eyes, his sight was restored, and he saw everything clearly.

MARK 8:22–25 ESV

Again desperate friends or family members brought a blind man to Jesus. The Master took him by the hand and led him apart from his friends. He spit on the man's eyes—for what reason no one knows—and laid hands on him. When He asked the man if he saw, he indicated partial vision—the only case in scripture in which Jesus did not heal someone immediately and fully. Scripture does not give us a reason for this gradual improvement.

But when Jesus touched him again, the healing was complete.

Do we doubt that Jesus can help us? Perhaps that's why we receive less than we expect from Him. Let's trust in Him and see marvelous things in our spiritual lives.

When he heard that it was Jesus of Nazareth,
he began to shout, "Jesus, Son of David, have mercy on me!"
Many rebuked him and told him to be quiet, but he shouted all
the more, "Son of David, have mercy on me!" . . . "What do you
want me to do for you?" Jesus asked him. The blind man said,
"Rabbi, I want to see." "Go," said Jesus, "your faith
has healed you." Immediately he received his sight
and followed Jesus along the road.

MARK 10:47–48, 51–52

Bartimaeus, a blind beggar, sat by the side of the road. Being unable to ply a trade, he made his living asking others for charity, a humiliating situation for anyone of this man's spirit.

Though he couldn't see, one day Bartimaeus heard a commotion going on and asked what it was. The people around him, probably the start of quite a crowd, answered that Jesus was coming by. The blind man immediately began shouting at the top of his lungs, "Jesus, Son of David, have mercy on me!" (10:47).

Those around the blind man began to take him to task. "Be quiet!" was probably the nicest rebuke he heard that day. But their discouragement just made the desperate man shout louder. Doubtless he wasn't at the front of the crowd, and he wanted Jesus to know he was there.

Jesus heard the hoopla and ordered His disciples to bring

the man to Him. "Cheer up! On your feet! He's calling you," they told Bartimaeus (10:49). The fearless man threw off his cloak, jumped to his feet, and came to Jesus.

When the Master asked what he wanted, Bartimaeus decisively told Him he wanted to see. No doubts in this man's mind or heart. He knew what he needed and had no qualms about asking for it. Jesus told him his faith had healed him.

The once-blind man immediately followed Jesus, praising God as he went. His joy was contagious, and others joined his praise party. Unlike some of those He healed, the Master did not tell him to stay at his home in Jericho. Can we doubt that He had a mission for Bartimaeus in the larger world?

Are we like blind Bartimaeus, sitting by the side of a spiritual road? If so, do we know what we want from Jesus, and are we unafraid to ask? The blind man's boldness brought him just the miracle he needed: His faith made him whole.

And Simon answered, "Master, we toiled all night
and took nothing! But at your word I will let down the nets."
And when they had done this, they enclosed a large number
of fish, and their nets were breaking.
LUKE 5:5–6 ESV

Pressured by the crowds surrounding Him, Jesus asked some fishermen for help. Peter and at least one more man (perhaps his brother, Andrew), who had probably been listening in on the Master's sermon, left their net washing to take Jesus on board. On the edge of the Sea of Galilee, their vessel became a temporary pulpit.

When Jesus finished teaching, He told Peter to go fishing. Though the fisherman had his doubts—he hadn't caught anything in a hard night's work—he headed for the deep water.

Peter caught so many fish his nets began to break. So he signaled his partners, James and John, to come help. As the second vessel came alongside, they tossed fish into that boat, too. And soon the two boats were all but overflowing.

Astonished at their catch, the fishermen knew what to make of it. Peter fell at the miracle-worker's feet and declared Him Lord.

We, too, see Jesus do astonishing things. How do we react? Will we call Him Lord, too?

A WONDROUS WORK

As he approached the town gate,
a dead person was being carried out—the only son of his
mother, and she was a widow. And a large crowd from the town
was with her. When the Lord saw her, his heart went out to her
and he said, "Don't cry." Then he went up and touched the coffin,
and those carrying it stood still. He said, "Young man, I say
to you, get up!" The dead man sat up and began to talk,
and Jesus gave him back to his mother.

LUKE 7:12–15

At Nain's gate, Jesus and the crowd around Him were met by a funeral cortege. The dead young man's mother, a widow, led the way to the burial place, with the men carrying her son's bier behind her. Surrounded by all her friends, family, and neighbors, she wept at the loss of her only son—the one she depended on for her support. For though a large crowd followed her today, where would they be for the rest of her life? At that moment, the widow's future looked rather grim.

Touched by her situation, the Lord approached and gently told her not to cry. She must have looked up at Him in shock. Her only son had died, and this stranger told her not to cry? If she shouldn't cry at this, what *should* she cry about?

But unlike some men, the Lord was not simply objecting because her tears made Him uncomfortable—He spoke the words from compassion. Jesus walked over to the bier her son lay on and touched it. Then He called the young man to arise.

Had the people of Nain heard of Jesus? Almost undoubtedly, since the city was in Galilee. Could they have known what to expect? No. This was the first of three resurrections Jesus performed during His ministry. Not since the days of the prophets Elijah and Elisha had humans returned from death at the touch of another human.

When the young man sat up, talking, Jesus returned him to his mother. Fear filled her eyes as she saw what Jesus had done, and the crowd about her feared, too. But their emotions turned to joy as they recognized the wondrous work of God among them.

Who could resist sharing this story? News of the event spread through the countryside. How many more people glorified God as they learned of this work?

When we hear of God's surprising work in another place, do we rejoice with those who have been blessed, or are we too busy gossiping about the story to recognize its importance? When one is healed, can we thankfully recognize the Great Physician's work in response to faithful prayer?

IN HIS NAME

After this the Lord chose seventy others.
He sent them out two together to every city and place where
He would be going later. . . . The seventy came back full
of joy. They said, "Lord, even the demons obeyed
us when we used Your name."
LUKE 10:1, 17 NLV

To further spread the ministry, Jesus sent about seventy men (some ancient manuscripts say seventy, some seventy-two) on a road trip. They went ahead of Him, in pairs, to prepare the way. If a town accepted them, they were to heal the ill there; if not, they were simply to leave.

This must have been an extraordinarily successful mission, since they reported that even those controlled by demons were cured when they healed in Jesus' name. Should the Seventy have been surprised? They'd seen Jesus perform numerous healings. But perhaps their amazement came because God had used *them*. Through their imperfect hands, Jesus had healed many more people than He personally could have touched in a day.

Like the Seventy, we are sinful humans to whom God has entrusted ministry. Despite our weaknesses, He works through our hands. Do we engage in that ministry reverently, aware of our own failings and humbled that God lets us work in His name?

FAITHFUL SAMARITAN, UNFAITHFUL JEWS

And as he entered a village, he was met by ten lepers,
who stood at a distance and lifted up their voices, saying,
"Jesus, Master, have mercy on us." When he saw them he
said to them, "Go and show yourselves to the priests."
And as they went they were cleansed.
LUKE 17:12–14 ESV

"Jesus, Master, have mercy on us." Jesus heard the cry as He entered the village, and off to one side stood ten lepers. Certainly they stood apart so as not to spread infection, but in that day they also would have been viewed as spiritually diseased. For in a day of limited medical knowledge, Jews saw this disease as a sign of God's displeasure. Their lives must have been a misery alleviated only by companionship with those who shared their impurity.

So when they heard that Jesus was coming to town, they banded together to seek healing. All He required of them was that they show themselves to the priests, whose job it was to check on such skin diseases and declare when a person was healed.

As the ten traveled to the priests, they received their healing, so they must have believed in Jesus and His powers. But we have to wonder just how grateful nine of them were for the healing. For only one of the ten returned to Jesus to report and appreciate. As he walked down the road toward

Jesus, the former leper praised God loudly. When he reached the Master, he fell at His feet and thanked Him.

Ironically, the single man who returned was a Samaritan, a race hated by the Jews because they had fallen into paganism. Yet the "good Jews" had not bothered to return to the One who healed them.

Jesus was not pleased at seeing only the one man. Though he who came could not be called an unbeliever now, he had not been born a Jew. Did Jesus' own people not appreciate what He had done?

We hear no more about the ungrateful nine. Perhaps they were still somewhat spiritually diseased, since praise and thankfulness did not return them to Jesus. But the single grateful man pierces our hearts as we read the story. Have we been guilty, like the missing nine, of ungratefulness? Are we faithful Samaritans or unfaithful Jews? Our level of thankfulness tells that to the Lord.

MERCY UNDER PRESSURE

When Jesus' disciples saw what was about to happen, they asked, "Lord, should we attack them with a sword?" One of the disciples even struck at the high priest's servant with his sword and cut off the servant's right ear. "Enough of that!" Jesus said. Then he touched the servant's ear and healed it.

LUKE 22:49–51 CEV

Judas led a crowd of Jesus' enemies, armed with swords and clubs, to the Garden of Gethsemane. There he betrayed the Master with a kiss. Though Jesus instantly recognized his intention, He did not fight back. He only tried to protect His disciples, asking that they be let go.

John tells us Peter was the one who tried to defend the Master by grabbing a sword and hacking off the ear of the high priest's servant, Malchus. Jesus rebuked Peter, pointing out that He could have called on the Father for protection, but scripture must be fulfilled (see Matthew 26:53). Then the Savior healed Malchus and demanded of His would-be attackers why they needed such force and stealth against someone who had been preaching publicly.

Even when Jesus was under the most pressure He'd confront in His earthly life, His forgiving nature demanded that He heal His enemy. How Malchus responded we do not know. But this story encourages us to forgive when we are oppressed. Will we offer healing to our enemies or begin a feud that can never end in peace?

WATER TO WINE

Jesus said to the servants, "Fill the jars with water."
And they filled them up to the brim. And he said to them,
"Now draw some out and take it to the master of the feast."
So they took it. When the master of the feast tasted the water
now become wine, and did not know where it came from
(though the servants who had drawn the water knew), the
master of the feast called the bridegroom and said to him,
"Everyone serves the good wine first, and when people
have drunk freely, then the poor wine. But you
have kept the good wine until now."

JOHN 2:7–10 ESV

Jesus' first miracle, described only in John's Gospel, took place at a wedding, quite possibly the wedding of one of His relatives. Along with His first-called disciples and His mother, He was invited. Legally, in that day, ten men were required to be at a wedding, and perhaps they invited Jesus and His disciples to make up six of that number.

This may not have been a very wealthy family, and though the guests may not have been numerous, the family was not too well prepared and ran out of wine. Weddings often went on for as much as a week. A poorer family might not celebrate all day long but would invite guests in for an evening meal each night. So running out of wine was a serious problem. Those who had enjoyed their friends' and neighbors' hospitality at their weddings committed a serious social faux pas by not returning their generosity—especially if those friends and neighbors were not well-to-do, either.

She wasn't in charge of the feast, but Mary came to her Son for a solution to the problem. Though she indirectly approached the issue, not actually asking Him to perform a miracle, she earned a mild rebuke, indicating she was not in charge of His messianic ministry. "Woman," He replied, using a term that was more respectful than it appears in English, "what does this have to do with me? My hour has not yet come" (2:4 ESV). Jesus indicated He was no longer under her authority, as He had been as a child. The ministry would be God directed, not ordered by His mama.

Mary simply left things to Jesus, ordering the servants to follow His direction. Doubtless, along with the rebuke was much affection. She must have understood this was not a firm dismissal of the need.

Six stone water jars, used for the Jewish purification rituals, stood nearby. Each held somewhere between twenty and thirty gallons. Jesus told the servants to fill each with water, and they filled them to the brim, losing no opportunity to be generous with the guests (and maybe to taste a little for themselves).

When they had hauled enough water to fill the jars, Jesus told them to give a cup to the banquet master. The master tasted it, unaware of where it had come from. Then he took the bridegroom aside and commended him on the wine. He simply wondered why they'd held on to the really good stuff until the end of the feast.

The water that became wine is symbolic on a number

of levels. First it represents the difference between the old and new covenants. But it also stands for the change in a new believer. The old spirit is gone, and the new one that replaces it has an unusual power, directly from God. A sinful existence, once so dull and unimportant, takes on a new life, verve, and significance.

What of our lives? Are they water or wine? Has God's Spirit filled us with the new life that enlivens like wine, or are we dull, ordinary water that lacks joy?

Even if we've come to know Jesus, if sin obstructs the Spirit's work in our lives, we may feel more like water than wine. Even the most faithful of us have dull days that are filled with obedience, but if every day seems dull, perhaps we need a little more of the Spirit's wine in our lives. If we cast aside anger, resentment, and bitterness, confessing our failures, the sparkle may come back. We don't have to live on a constant high, but the idea that God will use us for His purposes should cause within us a burst of joy, not a sigh of despair.

Today, are we water or wine?

WHOLE FAITH?

The man said to Him, "Sir, come with me before
my son dies." Jesus said to him, "Go your way. Your son will
live." The man put his trust in what Jesus said and left.
As he was on his way home, his servants met him.
They said to him, "Your son is living!"
JOHN 4:49–51 NLV

Sometime later, when Jesus returned to Cana, where he'd provided wine for the wedding feast, He was well received. But it wasn't because the Galileans believed in Him. Though He came from that part of Israel, they did not respect Him. They simply wanted to see more miracles.

When he heard that Jesus was nearby, a royal official came, asking Him to heal his son, who was dying of a fever. How desperate this man must have felt, yet Jesus did not jump up to follow him to his son's bedside. Instead, the Master confronted this "important" man with his need for signs and wonders.

The official persisted, asking Him to heal his son. So Jesus, probably tired of being appreciated only for entertainment value, compromised and healed the son without going to him.

The man proved he was not like the others, for he believed Jesus' promise of healing. While he was traveling home, his servants met him with joyous news: The boy lived. "When did he get better?" the official questioned his servants. They explained that the boy's fever left him at the seventh hour (one o'clock).

The trusting father realized that was just the time at which Jesus had spoken the words, "Your son will live." As they learned this, the official and his entire household believed.

Jesus was a man of His word. When He told a grieving father his child was healed, there was no question it had happened. But people are slow to realize that He is truthful above all others. The grieving father did well to trust as he walked home, but it was not until he learned the reality of his son's healing that the whole truth became apparent: Not only had his son been healed, but the man who healed him that was the Messiah.

Will we believe wholeheartedly, or is our faith all too partial? Jesus alone can be trusted to be all truth. Whom else could we turn to?

RULE FOLLOWER

The sick man answered Him,
"Sir, I have no man to put me into the pool when the water is
stirred up; but while I am coming, another steps down before
me." Jesus said to him, "Rise, take up your bed and walk."
And immediately the man was made well,
took up his bed, and walked.
JOHN 5:7–9 NKJV

On the Saturday Jesus visited the pool of Bethesda, many blind, lame, and paralyzed men, women, and children lay near the water, hoping for a miraculous cure. Jesus saw one man who probably looked as if he'd been around Bethesda's colonnaded porch a long time and asked about him. His was not some passing illness; he was an invalid. Someone reported he'd been so for thirty-eight years. Had he been lying near the pool every day for that time? Scripture never tells us. But we can be certain that doubt and depression had often filled his heart.

This day, Jesus asked if he wanted to be healed. Did the man jump at the chance? No. He carefully listed all the reasons why he couldn't be healed. Jesus did not rebuke his doubt; instead, He told him to get up, take his mat, and walk. And the man did just that. But as he walked away, some "holy" people asked what he was doing carrying a mat on the sabbath. He explained but could not name his healer. Later Jesus went to him and warned him to avoid sin, or worse would come upon him. Then the former invalid let the censorious Jews know His name.

This man was probably someone who played by the rules. He followed the healing rules, and he willingly informed on Jesus to the supposedly holy Jews who followed all the human laws Judaism had added to scripture. But these would-be holy ones missed out on the compassion that should have been part of their faith, and the healed man missed understanding that following all the rules had brought nothing; only when Jesus miraculously broke the laws of science could he walk.

Are we so busy following human rules that we miss out on understanding the Savior? Or are we taking scripture at its word and following closely in Jesus' steps?

So they took away the stone. And Jesus lifted up his eyes and said,
"Father, I thank you that you have heard me. I knew that you
always hear me, but I said this on account of the people standing
around, that they may believe that you sent me." When he
had said these things, he cried out with a loud voice, "Lazarus,
come out." The man who had died came out, his hands and feet
bound with linen strips, and his face wrapped with a cloth.
Jesus said to them, "Unbind him, and let him go."
JOHN 11:41–44 ESV

At first, when Lazarus got ill, no one may have thought it was a big deal. He'd get over it, with the best medical care available. Since he and his family were obviously well-to-do, getting good care would have been no problem. A visit to an apothecary would have provided medications. When things became more dire, a doctor could have been called in. This healer may even have gone to one of the best medical schools of his day. But obviously all the doctor's and apothecary's best efforts didn't work. Lazarus became weaker.

His sisters, Mary and Martha, knew how much Jesus loved their brother. They sent to Him, knowing He could heal Lazarus in a moment. But time went on, and the Master didn't come. Lazarus became even weaker and eventually died. His sisters, who loved him deeply, became distraught. Not only had they lost their brother, they could not understand why Jesus had failed them.

The grieving sisters buried their brother. Friends and neighbors surrounded them, but Jesus and His disciples remained absent. Several days after Lazarus's death, they still hadn't seen Him. Maybe a few wondered if the danger He was in from Jerusalem's religious leaders had kept Him far away. Since Bethany was a short trip from the capital city, had it been too close to those who hated Jesus?

Four days after the burial, five days from Lazarus's death, Jesus came. Somewhat gloomily, Martha told Him she knew that if He'd been there, her brother would not have died. Brightening a bit, she told Him of her trust that even now, God would do whatever He asked. Obviously she was hoping to see her brother again.

Jesus replied that her brother would rise again. Martha admitted she would see him in the resurrection on the last day, but she didn't admit she was hoping for something sooner than that.

"I am the resurrection and the life," Jesus reminded her (11:25 ESV). Death was not the end of the road for Lazarus, who had trusted in Him. The loving sister confessed Him as the Messiah and went to call her sister.

Mary came quickly to Jesus and repeated Martha's first words to Him, "Lord, if you had been here, my brother would not have died" (11:32 ESV). From neither sister did the Savior take offense. The two women did not lack faith, and perhaps they were stating fact, not rebuking Him. Their grief made them tenderly aware of Jesus' healing powers. Oh, that He had been there when Lazarus was so ill! Mary wept at the thought.

Jesus gently asked to see where Lazarus was laid—a normal request for a grieving friend. He wept on His way to His friend's resting place. The Jews (John only uses that term about Jesus' enemies) who had come to share the women's grief were amazed at Jesus' love for Lazarus, but some began to question why He hadn't healed one He loved so deeply.

When He came to the grave, Jesus asked that the stone be rolled away. Faithful Martha painfully reminded Him that by now her brother would be decomposing. "Did I not tell you that if you believed you would see the glory of God?" Jesus responded (11:40 ESV). Perhaps with a bit of hope, Martha commanded some men to move the stone.

Lifting His eyes to heaven, Jesus prayed, then commanded Lazarus to come forth from the tomb. He came out, the burial wrappings still surrounding his resurrected body. Jesus commanded his friends to unbind him, and what a celebration must have followed!

As a result of the miracle, many "Jews" believed in Jesus. But others reported the miracle to the Pharisees, who plotted to kill both Jesus and His resurrected friend.

We believe. Have we also seen the glory of God? Or do our own low expectations seem to limit the effectiveness of God's work in our lives? As He worked the most astounding miracle for the faithful sisters, Jesus will do so for us. He may not bring the physically dead back to life, but He'll work in our lives, if only we'll open the tomb door.

On the evening of that day, the first day of the week,
the doors being locked where the disciples were for fear of
the Jews, Jesus came and stood among them and said to them,
"Peace be with you." When he had said this, he showed them
his hands and his side. Then the disciples were glad when they
saw the Lord. Jesus said to them again, "Peace be with you.
As the Father has sent me, even so I am sending you."

JOHN 20:19–21 ESV

Following Jesus' death and even His resurrection, the disciples were holed up, trying to avoid His enemies. No question but that those unbelieving men would be angry at the news that all their efforts at ridding themselves of Jesus had been unsuccessful. But how long could the disciples remain in one place, keeping their heads low?

The evening of the day when Mary Magdalene and the other women had seen the resurrected Jesus, Jesus also appeared to ten of the Eleven. He didn't knock on their locked door, just appeared unexpectedly in the room they'd been sharing in their fear.

"Peace be with you," He greeted them. Then He proved He was no ghost, but the man they'd seen crucified, for He showed them all the signs of crucifixion upon Him—the marks of the nails in His hands and feet and the sword cut in His side. How delighted the disciples must have been to see Jesus. Perhaps they'd been wondering when He'd appear to them. After all, hadn't the women seen Him?

As the Father had sent Him, Jesus now sent the disciples to the world. He breathed on them, and they received the Holy Spirit. With His commission and the Spirit, they were ready to take on the world.

One of the Eleven was not with them—Thomas. When the others told him they'd seen the Lord, he would not believe. He wanted to see and judge for himself. Eight days later, Jesus reappeared in the same way. He encouraged Thomas to experience for himself the wounds that proved His had been a real resurrection. Jesus encouraged him, not in doubt but faith. Immediately Thomas recognized Him as Lord.

"Blessed," Jesus replied, "are those who have not seen and yet have believed" (20:29 ESV).

We, too, have been confronted with the Lord's resurrection. Have we believed? If He has breathed His Spirit upon us, we are ready for ministry. Will doubt delay us? We have no reason to wait.

GONE FISHING

Early in the morning Jesus stood on the shore of the lake.
The followers did not know it was Jesus. Then Jesus said to them,
"Children, do you have any fish?" They said, "No." He said to
them, "Put your net over the right side of the boat. Then you
will catch some fish." They put out the net. They were
not able to pull it in because it was so full of fish.
JOHN 21:4–6 NLV

Perhaps feeling a little bit at a loss after the Resurrection, Peter decided to go night fishing. Thomas, Nathanael, James, and John joined him; arduous work was better than idle waiting. All night the men floated on the Sea of Galilee, working hard but catching nothing.

About the time tempers were probably getting short, early the next morning they saw a figure on the shore. "Children, do you have any fish?" the man asked (21:5 NLV). When they replied in the negative, He told them to put their net over on the right side of their vessel and promised they'd make a catch.

Fishermen of that day often used spotters, who stood on the shore and directed the men in the boat to the schools of fish. But what a catch they hauled in this time—they couldn't pull the net in because it was so full. Muscles aching, John finally realized who that spotter had been. "It is the Lord!" he cried (21:7 NLV).

Enthusiastic Peter leapt into the water and headed for

the shore, with the other disciples following in the boat. When they got to shore, they found a fire, ready to cook a fish breakfast. Though they'd caught 153 fish, their nets were undamaged.

None of us enjoy waiting for God. We want to be on the move with ministry, making ourselves worthwhile. But sometimes we run headlong into God's plan, which requires us to wait patiently while other things resolve themselves. As we wait, we too may go fishing, returning to ordinary tasks. Though God abundantly blesses these, we need to stand ready for His call to return to our work for Him. Are we ready to drop our nets and take up His work today?

MORE THAN WIND

When the day of Pentecost arrived,
they were all together in one place. And suddenly
there came from heaven a sound like a mighty rushing wind,
and it filled the entire house where they were sitting.
And divided tongues as of fire appeared to them and rested
on each one of them. And they were all filled with the
Holy Spirit and began to speak in other tongues
as the Spirit gave them utterance.
ACTS 2:1–4 ESV

Fifty days after Passover, the Eleven and probably 120 other Christians (see verse 5) gathered for the Jewish feast of Pentecost. It may have seemed an ordinary feast day, but suddenly, a rushing wind filled the house and tongues of fire rested on every person present. All were filled with the Holy Spirit and began speaking in foreign tongues, whether or not they had ever known how to speak them before!

Hearing these Christians, devout Jews came to see what was going on and heard them speaking their own languages—for many foreign-language speakers either lived in the capital city or had gathered from other parts of the world to celebrate Pentecost. They all marveled at the event. Yet a few unbelievers tried to blame it on too much wine.

Peter preached a sermon, explaining that Old Testament prophecies had been fulfilled, and God's Spirit now indwelled those who believed in Jesus. That day, about three thousand more believed in Him anew.

The Holy Spirit may not come to us in a whoosh of wind, and we may never wear a tongue of fire, but He works within our hearts when we accept His power and trust in Jesus. He is more than wind in our lives—He fills our spirits and leads us in God's truth, if only we open ourselves to Him.

POINTING TO JESUS

But Peter said, "I have no silver and gold,
but what I do have I give to you. In the name of Jesus Christ
of Nazareth, rise up and walk!" And he took him by the right
hand and raised him up, and immediately his feet and ankles
were made strong. And leaping up he stood and began
to walk, and entered the temple with them,
walking and leaping and praising God.
ACTS 3:6–8 ESV

Peter and John were headed for the temple one afternoon for prayer when some men carried a crippled man to the most popular gate of the worship center. There he earned a living by begging for alms from worshipers.

As he did with everyone else, the man begged for some of the apostles' loose change. But Peter was about to give him something much, much better. He engaged the man's attention and told him he had no gold. Then he commanded the man to walk in the name of Jesus. Taking the beggar by one hand, the apostle lifted him to his feet. In an instant, the man's feet and ankles became strong. He jumped up and walked, following the apostles into the temple courts.

When worshipers recognized the healed man, they were amazed. Peter, ever the preacher, took the opportunity to point them to Jesus.

Do we take every opportunity to point people to Jesus? Let's not ignore His Spirit's call.

But Peter said, "Ananias, why has Satan filled
your heart to lie to the Holy Spirit and keep back part
of the price of the land for yourself? . . . You have not lied to
men but to God." Then Ananias, hearing these words, fell
down and breathed his last. . . . "Look, the feet of those who
have buried your husband are at the door, and they will carry
you out." Then immediately [Sapphira] fell down at his feet and
breathed her last. And the young men came in and found her
dead, and carrying her out, buried her by her husband.
ACTS 5:3–5, 9–10 NKJV

Generosity filled the young church when Barnabas sold some land so that he could offer the money to the apostles. But one couple didn't quite get the point of this kind of giving. They saw Barnabas give unreservedly and heard other church members sing his praises. Together they decided they'd like that kind of recognition, but not at the price Barnabas had paid. The couple decided to sell a spare piece of property and give money to the church. But why should they lose everything? They'd give Peter only part of the cash.

If they'd stopped there, it would have been fine. But the couple led everyone to believe they'd given the whole price of the land.

When they brought the offering before Peter, he was incensed. He didn't care if they'd only given a certain amount to the church—but to claim one thing and do another was another matter. He indicted Ananias with his words, indicating he knew what they'd done. He informed them that the couple had lied to God, not man.

Ananias fell down and died when he heard the apostle's words. Men came forward and buried him immediately.

Later, Ananias's wife, Sapphira, came in. Peter asked her about the price they'd paid for the land, and she too lied. She quickly followed her husband to the grave. Fear filled the church when people found out about these events.

Do we lie to God? Let's remember the ending of this story and reconsider all we say and do.

SIGNS AND WONDERS

And through the hands of the apostles many signs and wonders were done among the people. . . . They brought the sick out into the streets and laid them on beds and couches, that at least the shadow of Peter passing by might fall on some of them. Also a multitude gathered from the surrounding cities to Jerusalem, bringing sick people and those who were tormented by unclean spirits, and they were all healed.

ACTS 5:12, 15–16 NKJV

The Jewish people might have gotten somewhat used to Jesus' miracles, but their astonishment peaked again, after His death, when they discovered the miracles had not ended. Though Jesus no longer walked among them, the apostles did. And from them proceeded amazing signs and wonders.

Is it any wonder that the people thought well of the Eleven? Even the religious authorities did not keep them from meeting in the temple.

When they saw the miracles, many came to believe in Jesus, and others, even those from outside Jerusalem, brought the sick and those afflicted with evil spirits. They placed them on the cots and mats in the street, hoping Peter's shadow would fall over them and they would be healed. In His mercy, God caused them all to return to health.

God is more willing to do miracles in our lives than we might expect. Are we in a humble spiritual state in which He can bless us?

PUBLIC ENEMY NUMBER ONE

*But Saul, still breathing threats and murder against the
disciples of the Lord, went to the high priest and asked him for
letters to the synagogues at Damascus, so that if he found any
belonging to the Way, men or women, he might bring them
bound to Jerusalem. Now as he went on his way, he approached
Damascus, and suddenly a light from heaven flashed around
him. And falling to the ground he heard a voice saying to him,
"Saul, Saul, why are you persecuting me?" And he said, "Who are
you, Lord?" And he said, "I am Jesus, whom you are persecuting.
But rise and enter the city, and you will be told what you are
to do." . . . Saul rose from the ground, and although his eyes
were opened, he saw nothing. So they led him by the hand
and brought him into Damascus. And for three days he
was without sight, and neither ate nor drank.*

Acts 9:1–6, 8–9 esv

Public Enemy Number One: that's what the Pharisee
Saul started out being to first-century Christians. He had
approved of and even taken part in Stephen's stoning. Then
he'd persecuted Christians, sending them to prison. As a
result, many believers left Jerusalem to settle elsewhere.

One day, on His way to Damascus to expand his persecu-
tion of Christians, Saul was traveling unconcernedly when a
heavenly light flashed around him. He fell to the ground and
heard a voice asking, "Saul, Saul, why are you persecuting me?"
(verse 4 esv). Because he couldn't see anything, Saul asked who

was speaking to him. That's when he learned it was Jesus—a shocking discovery indeed.

The voice told him to rise and enter Damascus. Saul started to obey, but he could not move ahead on his own: He was completely blind. The men who traveled with them had heard the mysterious voice but could not understand it (see 22:9). They stood speechless, seeing no one. But when Saul rose, they took him by the hand and brought him into the city.

For three days, the sightless Saul fasted and prayed. This sudden, enforced retreat was designed to make him rethink his opinion of Jesus and His people. During those days, a Christian named Ananias (obviously not Sapphira's husband but a man of Damascus) had a vision. God told him to go to Straight Street and look for Saul of Tarsus (see 9:11).

This was not news Ananias wanted to hear. He quickly recognized the name of the man he was to visit. His response was something like, "Lord, are You kidding? Do You remember how dangerous this guy is? He might decide he wants to throw me in prison, like a lot of the other Christians he's run into. And the chief priests think he's the greatest thing since challah bread!"

But the Lord repeated His command to go. He shared that He was about to turn Saul so far around that he'd become a missionary to the Gentiles.

Comforted, Ananias went to Straight Street. He laid hands on the former Public Enemy Number One and told him that Jesus had sent him. Saul was to receive his sight back and be filled with the Holy Spirit (9:17).

Something like scales fell from Saul's eyes, and he could see again. He arose, received baptism, and ate again (9:18–19). Then he set off on his mission, first meeting with the disciples in the city, then preaching in the Damascene synagogues. Everyone there was amazed at Saul's change of heart, and his powerful preaching turned hearts toward Jesus (9:20–22).

When we speak of conversions, we often think of Saul's dramatic experience. And for many of us, that seems to be the way that leads to Christ. Suddenly, we recognize our own sin and fall on the tarmac before Him. But other Christians have a quiet or slowly increasing conviction that He is Lord. However we come to Jesus, He transforms our lives if we are willing to make them a mission for Him. Whether we fall down on the road to Damascus or simply feel the still, small voice that leads us into faith, we will never be the same. New life is a sign of new faith.

Now as Peter went here and there among them all,
he came down also to the saints who lived at Lydda. There
he found a man named Aeneas, bedridden for eight years, who
was paralyzed. And Peter said to him, "Aeneas, Jesus Christ
heals you; rise and make your bed." And immediately he rose.
And all the residents of Lydda and Sharon saw him,
and they turned to the Lord.

ACTS 9:32–35 ESV

Aeneas had lain in bed for eight years, paralyzed. As the apostle Peter went about his work for the Lord, overseeing church growth, he came into Aeneas's hometown of Lydda. Perhaps the town gossips had told Aeneas about the healings that had taken place in Jerusalem. Or maybe a relative or friend went to Peter to call him to the paralyzed man's bedside. Whatever caused the apostle to come there, it was a wonderful time for Aeneas. No doctor could help him. This was his only hope.

Of course, Peter did not take the credit for himself. He healed the man in the name of Jesus and told him to rise and make his bed. Aeneas couldn't jump up fast enough! The healed man must have spread his joy not only through his community but to those all around, because the residents of both Lydda and the Plain of Sharon saw him walking and turned to his Lord.

We, too, have a testimony. Will our energy for Jesus draw others to Him?

Peter sent them all out of the room; then he got down on his knees and prayed. Turning toward the dead woman, he said, "Tabitha, get up." She opened her eyes, and seeing Peter she sat up. He took her by the hand and helped her to her feet. Then he called the believers and the widows and presented her to them alive. This became known all over Joppa, and many people believed in the Lord.

ACTS 9:40–42

Farther along the Plain of Sharon lay Joppa. When word came that Peter was in nearby Lydda, the Christians of this seaport town sent to ask him to come. One of their members, Tabitha (her name in Aramaic) or Dorcas (a Greek translation of her name), who delighted in doing good works for the church, had died. Her body had been washed for burial, but before they went further, the Christians sent two men to Lydda to ask the apostle to come to her aid. Peter accompanied these messengers back to their city.

In an upper room, the other widows showed him all the garments she had made for them. But Peter wasn't interested in a fashion show. He put them gently out of the room, prayed, and called Tabitha's name, telling her to arise. Opening her eyes and sitting up, she looked at the apostle. He took her hand, raised her out of the bed, and called in the other Christians, who were probably waiting anxiously on the lower floor.

The story of her return to life must have flown around the town, and surely people came to see her with their own eyes. When they saw what had happened and heard her testimony, it certainly caused them to think. Since the apostle stayed for some time in the city, they must also have heard his preaching. As a result of this miracle, many came to know the Lord.

Tabitha's good works did not end with making clothes, a time-consuming effort in the days before sewing machines. Obviously she allowed her new life, following her death, to shine as brightly as her good works had before Peter came to raise her. Because she had a consistent Christian walk, people could believe in her resurrection and the Lord who had been behind the miracle.

Will our lives show forth God's truth this clearly? All we do out of love for Him can serve to make His name known. When we need to shine out brightly for Him, will we be ready to do so?

WITNESSING WELL

In Lystra there sat a man crippled in his feet,
who was lame from birth and had never walked.
He listened to Paul as he was speaking. Paul looked
directly at him, saw that he had faith to be healed and
called out, "Stand up on your feet!" At that,
the man jumped up and began to walk.
ACTS 14:8–10

This unnamed man of Lystra, a Galatian city, had never effectively set foot on earth. With no wheelchairs available, moving him from one place to another must have been a chore. Yet when Paul and Barnabas spoke in his city, he was there, ears and heart wide open.

Paul noticed the man and studied him for a bit before he spoke out, calling the cripple to stand. The man energetically sprang up and began walking.

The watching crowd immediately came to the wrong conclusion: They decided Barnabas and Paul were gods and started to call for sacrifices to be made to them. The anguished apostles spoke out, witnessing about the Lord, and just barely stopped the sacrifices from taking place.

Sometimes we witness and people come to the wrong conclusion. Like Paul and Barnabas, we need to make efforts to redirect their thinking into a better way. Can we explain Christ to people in a number of ways so they can clearly understand who He is?

DEMONIC AFFLICTION

As we were going to the place of prayer,
we were met by a slave girl who had a spirit of divination
and brought her owners much gain by fortune-telling. She
followed Paul and us, crying out, "These men are servants of
the Most High God, who proclaim to you the way of salvation."
And this she kept doing for many days. Paul, having become
greatly annoyed, turned and said to the spirit, "I command
you in the name of Jesus Christ to come out of her."
And it came out that very hour.
ACTS 16:16–18 ESV

In Acts, Luke tells this story that took place in the Macedonian city of Philippi, as a slave girl filled with a demonic spirit spoke out occult oracles.

Paul and his companions, including Luke, may have met for prayer outside the city because their religion was considered a strange cult by the Philippians and therefore could not be practiced inside the municipality. On their way to the prayer place near the river, they met this slave girl, who was filled with an irritating spirit that pestered Paul by declaring that he and his friends served the Most High God. A Jew might properly have understood that description, but there were few Jews in the city, which numbered many former Roman soldiers in its population. Most of the people in Philippi held to some sort of pagan belief and probably would have thought the phrase referred to the god Zeus. Then as now, Satan could mislead with crafty words; even when he spoke the truth, it could lead people in the wrong direction.

Greek religion had a mishmash of influences. Cults from all over the Near East had influenced this pagan faith. Magic and sorcery were popular methods people tried to use to understand an often confusing world. The kind of spirit this girl was afflicted with is described as a *python*, the same kind of spirit that supposedly gave visions to the Greek oracle at Delphi. This pagan priestess was consulted by Greek rulers and common people alike and responded to them in riddles. (That way the recipient could always assume: The oracle was right. I just didn't understand what she said.)

Naturally, Paul did not appreciate the slave girl's running commentary, especially when it led people away from Christ. After many days of patiently putting up with her, Paul had had enough. He commanded the spirit to come out of her.

Though that cleansing freed the servant girl from the demon, it brought the wrath of her owners down on Paul's head. No longer could she earn plenty of money by telling people's fortunes—her owners had lost a valuable commodity. And someone was going to pay. The owners dragged Paul and Silas in front of the authorities.

"They advocate customs that are not lawful for us as Romans to accept or practice," the irate owners claimed about Paul and his disciples (16:21 ESV). Philippi was a Roman colony and proud of its connection with the Italian city. It didn't hurt their case to claim that these outlanders were running counter to the Roman way of life and were a danger to the city. But in reality, they wanted their oracle back.

As a result, Paul and Silas spent an eventful night in jail. First they were beaten. Then at midnight the foundations of their place of incarceration were shattered by an earthquake. Their testimony converted the jailer, and in the end, at Paul's insistence, the city magistrates led them honorably out of the jail.

Do we recognize the joys of knowing Jesus? Let's think what it would be like to live a pagan lifestyle. The slave girl didn't experience joy, for a demon directed all she did. Even those who did not have a demon within lived without security, seeing themselves as being at the whim of gods whose minds changed constantly.

Maybe their lives aren't so different from today's unbelievers who suffer the same doubts and troubles. Can we have compassion on them and seek to separate them from their demonic afflictions?

AN EXTRAORDINARY PATH

God did extraordinary miracles through Paul,
so that even handkerchiefs and aprons that had touched
him were taken to the sick, and their illnesses
were cured and the evil spirits left them.
ACTS 19:11–12

The apostle Peter's shadow was sought for its healing properties (see Acts 5:12, 15–16), but with Paul, people looked to fabric that had touched him to heal their bodies and souls.

While he preached in Corinth with Priscilla and Aquila, Paul had returned to his trade as a tentmaker. He must have continued his trade, for somehow, when he moved on to Ephesus, the items he used as protection or for personal comfort as he worked began to be valued by those seeking healing.

These were not ordinary miracles, and they certainly did not follow any previous pattern, but God graciously used even these common items to bring healing to those who sought Paul out.

Ephesus was the most important city in Asia Minor, both politically and commercially. Worship of the fertility goddess Artemis made the local idol makers successful. So it's not surprising that the outcome of the healings associated with Paul stirred up dissatisfaction in that quarter. A riot resulted, which caused Paul to move on to Macedonia.

Are we willing to give our lives to Jesus and let Him

do as He wills with them? Maybe He will send us down an extraordinary path. Are we willing to go wherever He calls us?

DEVOTED TO THE WORD

Seated in a window was a young man named Eutychus, who was sinking into a deep sleep as Paul talked on and on. When he was sound asleep, he fell to the ground from the third story and was picked up dead. Paul went down, threw himself on the young man and put his arms around him. "Don't be alarmed," he said. "He's alive!" Then he went upstairs again and broke bread and ate. After talking until daylight, he left.

ACTS 20:9–11

Paul came to the city of Troas for a brief visit. No doubt the believers there were well aware they needed to make the most of the time they had with him. On his last night there, a crowd of folks must have been ready to hear his preaching, because young Eutychus ended up sitting in a window. Or perhaps the air was cooler there, so he chose the precarious place. Though the sill may have been broad and seemed safe enough, perhaps the young freedman had had a long day and underestimated how tired he'd feel after Paul had talked for a while. Unwilling to miss anything, the young Christian remained, growing ever sleepier.

Though Paul was planning to travel the next day, he was anxious to share as much as possible with the fledgling congregation. He kept preaching late into the night, by lamplight. Around midnight, it all became too much for Eutychus. He fell sound asleep. Since the Christians were meeting in a third-floor room, the sleeping man fell headlong to the ground and was killed.

The believers of Troas, seeing and hearing him fall, hurried to help their brother. Quickly Paul appeared beside them. The apostle threw himself on Eutychus and took him in his arms. "Don't be alarmed," he comforted the grieving Christians, "he's alive."

Obviously, the Christians of Troas had had time enough to check things out and know Eutychus had not been living when they first came to him. A rare kind of miracle had occurred right before their eyes.

Paul returned to the room and began to serve the Lord's Supper to the no-doubt-excited congregation. Then he ate a late dinner and talked with the congregation until daybreak.

We've all listened to long, and possibly even dull, sermons. We can feel for this young man as his head nods. But have we been so devoted to hearing the Word that we were willing to stay under less than comfortable circumstances? Let's avoid his foolhardiness even as we share Eutychus's devotion to God's Word.

SNAKE ESCAPE

*Paul gathered a pile of brushwood and, as he put it
on the fire, a viper, driven out by the heat, fastened itself
on his hand. When the islanders saw the snake hanging
from his hand, they said to each other, "This man must be a
murderer; for though he escaped from the sea, Justice has not
allowed him to live." But Paul shook the snake off into the fire
and suffered no ill effects. The people expected him to swell up
or suddenly fall dead, but after waiting a long time and
seeing nothing unusual happen to him, they changed
their minds and said he was a god.*

ACTS 28:3–6

Paul and his companions were sailing to Rome when their vessel was shipwrecked; after an eventful night on the sea, they landed on the Island of Malta. The people of the island, having seen the wreck, came to their aid, building a fire to warm the survivors. Ever helpful, the apostle set himself to gathering wood to feed the fire. But when he put the sticks on it, a viper, attempting to escape the flames, grabbed on to Paul's hand.

The snake must have been a poisonous one, for as soon as they saw this, the islanders assumed Paul was a dead man. Knowing he was a Roman prisoner, they assumed he was a murderer and that though he'd escaped drowning, he would now receive his just reward.

Imagine their shock when Paul shook off the snake

and went on as before. Instead of falling dead, he remained perfectly healthy. Instead, they decided he must be a god.

Maybe we'd better not fool with poisonous snakes and assume God will keep us alive. But we can praise Him that He gave everyone this impressive sign of His power.

WELCOME GUESTS

There was an estate nearby that belonged to Publius, the chief official of the island. He welcomed us to his home and for three days entertained us hospitably. His father was sick in bed, suffering from fever and dysentery. Paul went in to see him and, after prayer, placed his hands on him and healed him. When this had happened, the rest of the sick on the island came and were cured. They honored us in many ways and when we were ready to sail, they furnished us with the supplies we needed.
ACTS 28:7–10

After Paul proved he was no murderer, the chief official on Malta, Publius, invited Paul and his companion Luke into his home. Perhaps others joined them, too. But Paul must have made the greatest impression on the official, because when he discovered that Publius's father was suffering from fever and dysentery, the apostle went to see what he could do. He came to the man, prayed, and placed his hands on him to heal him.

When the people of the island saw what Paul had done,

they brought the sick to him, and they also were cured. As Paul and his companion left, the island dwellers honored them greatly and gave them all the supplies they'd need for their travel. Their original fear, that Paul was a dangerous murderer, had disappeared.

Paul made himself and Luke very welcome guests, for they did what they could to help their host. We may not be able to heal the ill, but we can defy Benjamin Franklin's idea that after three days, fish and guests stink. May we serve, not expect to be served, wherever we go.

These men have power to shut up the sky so that it will not rain during the time they are prophesying; and they have power to turn the waters into blood and to strike the earth with every kind of plague as often as they want. Now when they have finished their testimony, the beast that comes up from the Abyss will attack them, and overpower and kill them. Their bodies will lie in the street of the great city. . . . For three and a half days men from every people, tribe, language and nation will gaze on their bodies and refuse them burial. The inhabitants of the earth will gloat over them and will celebrate by sending each other gifts, because these two prophets had tormented those who live on the earth. But after the three and a half days a breath of life from God entered them, and they stood on their feet, and terror struck those who saw them. Then they heard a loud voice from heaven saying to them, "Come up here." And they went up to heaven in a cloud, while their enemies looked on.

REVELATION 11:6–12

In the book of Revelation, God gave the apostle John a prophetic vision concerning two miraculous witnesses who, at the end time, will prophesy for 1,260 days.

John's description of these future events reminds us of numerous Old Testament passages. He describes the two men as olive trees and lampstands. Though scholars disagree about whether these are two actual people or symbolic figures who stand for the church, and though they debate when these two will appear, there is no question that when we see miraculous events that remind us of Elijah and Moses, we'll know the events John prophesied are taking place. Under the prophets' command rain will stop and the waters turn to blood. Through them, people will be struck with plagues.

Once their testimony is done, the demonic beast will attack and destroy them, but only in a temporary, earthly sense. Their bodies will remain unburied—a great insult in the first-century world and a horror to us today—and many of their enemies come to gawk. Though victory holds off, three days later, like Jesus, God will raise them back to life. Then He'll call His faithful witnesses to Himself in eternity, and they'll rise up into heaven in a cloud. When the prophets' enemies see what happens, terror will strike them.

As the prophets leave earth, the city (variously described by scholars as Jerusalem, Rome, or another evil city) will experience an earthquake that will kill seven thousand people and terrify the rest into worshiping the Lord.

What do these prophecies symbolize? It isn't the most detailed description, and as we read, it leaves us with many unanswered questions. Let's take comfort in the fact that we have plenty of company—both scholars and lay Christians have doubts about what the Revelation means. We all read it carefully, but none of us understands it completely.

When we read the book of Revelation, we are in the same position Old Testament believers who studied the messianic prophecies were in: We can't clearly see what God's Word means, and we cannot accurately predict how it will work out. Just as the ancient Israelites read the Prophets and trusted that Jesus would come, we need to keep our minds open to see God's outworking of His prophecy. Jesus did not come exactly the way people in the first century expected, and it's likely God will have a few surprises for us, too. But as we look ahead to the fulfillment of New Testament prophecy, we know that God will fulfill His will. All we need to do is continue to seek Him.

In the meantime, let's not become too certain we know just what God plans as He begins to close out this earthly life, or we might be looking in the wrong direction when He comes.

Then I saw a new heaven and a new earth,
for the first heaven and the first earth had passed away,
and there was no longer any sea. I saw the Holy City, the new
Jerusalem, coming down out of heaven from God, prepared
as a bride beautifully dressed for her husband. And I heard a
loud voice from the throne saying, "Now the dwelling of God is
with men, and he will live with them. They will be his people,
and God himself will be with them and be their God. He
will wipe every tear from their eyes. There will be no
more death or mourning or crying or pain, for the
old order of things has passed away."
REVELATION 21:1–4

While many prophetic passages in Revelation cause us to question, this one simply brings us much courage and hope. As we look at the Bible's final miracle, our hearts lift up. For the sins and hardships of this world will not last forever. Everything we know now will be erased, and God will provide a beautiful Jerusalem without sin or stain. There He will live with us, and no one will cry over death or anything else. We will endlessly know the joy of living with Jesus forever.

Today, when life is hard or we don't see the purpose in our Christian lives, we can look forward to the last miracle God will perform on earth. It's a miracle that renews the earth—and renews us, too. For we will be without sin, living with Him eternally.

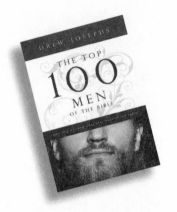
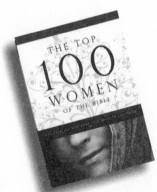